—

REASONABLE DOUBTS

REASONABLE DOUBTS

A RELIGIOUS SKEPTIC
LEARNS
A THING OR TWO
ABOUT GOD

CHERYL BERMAN

URIM PUBLICATIONS
JERUSALEM • NEW YORK

Reasonable Doubts:
A Religious Skeptic Learns A Thing Or Two About God
by Cheryl Berman

Copyright © 2010 by Cheryl Berman

Printed in Israel
First Edition

ISBN 978-965-524-039-9

Urim Publications, P.O. Box 52287, Jerusalem 91521 Israel
Typeset by Ariel Walden

Lambda Publishers Inc.
3709 13th Avenue Brooklyn, New York 11218 U.S.A.
Tel: 718-972-5449 Fax: 718-972-6307, mh@ejudaica.com

www.UrimPublications.com

This book is dedicated to those who doubt . . . and then doubt themselves.

ACKNOWLEDGEMENTS

THIS BOOK HAS benefited from so many different voices, and I am deeply grateful to each and every one.

First and foremost I wish to express my gratitude to God for providing me with this poignant life experience and the voice with which to speak about it.

I want to thank my children Avi, Devora, Tani, and Noa who serve as a living reminder that the hidden miracles of God are no less miraculous than the overt ones. I also wish to thank my husband, Moshe. Finding someone who understands you better than you understand yourself is in itself no small miracle.

I would like to thank my parents, Rosalie and Ted Berman, for being an enduring source of support and love.

My deepest gratitude goes to Dr. David Shatz who agreed to read and comment on my manuscript. Dr. Shatz has always served as a model of someone who balances an extensive knowledge of philosophy with a steadfast unyielding faith, and that has helped me immensely during the bleakest hours of my faith crisis.

Many family members and friends volunteered to read and comment on my manuscript. I want to thank Alex Berman, Shevi Berman, Ari Berman, Anita Berman, Mali Brofsky, Dr. Yoel Finkelman, Fred Levi, Rena Levi, Gert Sternfield, and Daniel Teichman for all of their incisive feedback.

Dena Blank provided me with helpful publishing and marketing advice, and Gila Green did a meticulous job editing my manuscript. Sara Eisen was the hand that held I held and the ear that I sought throughout writing, editing, and publication of the book. I could not have found a better writer, editor, or friend to walk me through this. Thank you.

I want to thank Shoshana Teichman for her breathtaking cover design. I also wish to acknowledge Tzvi Mauer and the entire Urim staff for working tirelessly and professionally to get my book into print.

Finally, I want to thank you, dear reader. I started this project with the intent of helping people who are going through a crises of faith. But in the process of writing this book I have uncovered countless insights regarding myself and my relationship with my Creator. I have you to thank for that.

—Cheryl Berman

CONTENTS

Dear Reader,

This book does not seek to present you with intellectual proofs for the existence of God. I'll leave that to the philosophers. This book does not attempt to investigate the true nature of God. I'll leave that to the mystics. This book is simply the story of one woman's attempt to understand.

—Cheryl Berman

❀ Skepticism is the beginning of faith

— Oscar Wilde
(*The Picture of Dorian Gray*, Chapter 17)

Pain and Parchment

Sixth Century BCE, a village in the Valley of the Rivers of Chebar, Babylonia

ELIHU RUBBED HIS burning eyes with one hand, as he reached for his scroll with the other. He had been having a difficult time getting his former home in Jerusalem out of his mind. The thoughts had become an unwelcome intruder encroaching on his daily life. He would be involved in some innocuous undertaking, eating or writing letters perhaps, when visions of the Jewish Holy Temple would invade his consciousness.

He would remember the way the Levites would greet the harried worshipers with the soothing strum of their instruments. He would remember the look of intense concentration on the High Priest's face as he carried the incense to the most sacred room in the Temple on Yom Kippur, knowing that the slightest break in momentum might mean death for himself and the nation. He would remember the delight and the unity of his people when they gathered three times a year in the Temple to serve God.

That's when his eyes would sting the most: when he thought of the mirth of his people. He sighed deeply and grabbed his parchment. He needed to heal them. He needed to answer their unspoken grief. He needed to speak to his people.

The Babylonian exile took the Jewish people away from their Temple.

The Babylonians took the Temple away from God. And now the people were left bereft of their unity and their joy. They had no soft music to settle their minds. They had nowhere to gather three times a year. The High Priest had no more role to play, and the people yearned for his spiritual guidance. The people needed to know how God could let this happen. Why had God forsaken them?

There were prophets in the town squares addressing the people's questions. The prophets spoke of sin and desecration of God. But Elihu knew this wasn't the whole story. There had to be more. Sin might explain national suffering, but it couldn't explain individual suffering. Sin might explain taking the Temple from the *people*, but it couldn't explain taking the Temple from the *person*. Sin might explain the exile, but it couldn't explain the burning in Elihu's eyes.

So Elihu undertook the explanation himself. He decided to tell a tale. It would be a tale of seemingly innocent suffering. It would be a tale about challenging God. It would be a tale that asks more questions than it answers. And he would call it the *Book of Job*.

PART ONE

CHAPTER ONE

The Ghost of Immanuel Kant

"SCIENCE IS WHAT you know, philosophy is what you don't know." It sounds like something a scientist might say to taunt a philosopher over the course of a heated argument. But it isn't. It is statement made by the twentieth-century British philosopher Bertrand Russell. But what was Russell's point? I could understand involving yourself in a field whose object is knowable. But what would be the purpose of enveloping yourself in the unknowable? The question reminds me of a conversation I had with a friend of mine. She had almost completed medical school and I was still in graduate school studying medieval Jewish philosophy. "Cheryl, can I ask you a question?" She inquired.

"Sure," I replied unsuspectingly.

"Well, I don't mean to insult you but . . . what is taking you so long? I mean I'm studying medicine which is something you can actually use in life. You are studying . . . what are you studying again?"

"Medieval Jewish philosophy," I responded, pretty sure about where this conversation was going.

"Yeah, well, you aren't really studying anything you could do something with, so why is it taking so long?"

I wasn't completely sure of the connection between the utility of a field and the length of time it took to acquire knowledge of it. I *could* have said something like, "Well, I've only completed two out of three of my language requirements: classical Arabic and French. How many language requirements did you have again? Oh that's right . . . none." I *should* have said, "Science is what you know, philosophy is what you don't know. Clearly we know a lot less than what we don't know, so it's taking me longer to complete my studies." But what I *actually* said was, "You're right. I don't know why it's taking so long." And I hung up the phone feeling a bit like someone had just insulted my mother.

Philosophers are hyper-aware that the subject of their field is essentially a non-entity. Philosophers deal with questions, thoughts, ideas. The clay of science is an object, an experience, a phenomenon; the clay of philosophy is questions about the clay itself. Where did it come from? Was it created or was it always there? What purpose does it serve, if any? And of course, what role do I serve in relation to this clay? Questions. That's all philosophers deal with. Philosophers know this. But they also know that when you really think about it, questions might be all there is.

Philosophers have made their livings challenging some basic assumptions. The eighteenth-century Scottish philosopher David Hume, for example, was famous for reinterpreting the principle of cause and effect. He pointed out that the notion of cause and effect is based on a construct of the human mind. People see two events occurring consecutively and draw the conclusion that one event caused the other. For example, if my finger accidentally comes in contact with a burning hot stove and I get a painful burn, I draw the conclusion that my finger touching the hot stove caused the burn. But in reality I have simply witnessed two events occurring successively; I noticed that my finger grazed the stove and then I saw that my finger was burned. I induce from those two consecutive events that the stove caused the burn. But that is just an induction, a creation of my mind that I used to explain the burn. In principle, tomorrow I might touch the same burning hot stove and my hand won't be affected at all. Are basic principles of physics -- like cause and effect – actually rules that are somehow embedded into the fabric of our universe? Or are they simply constructs of our own minds that we use to understand the world around us? More Questions.

The seventeenth-century French philosopher Rene Descartes went a step further. He challenged our most basic assumption: the existence of the physical world. We all have had the experience of a dream that seemed to be real. Who is to say, he argued, that we aren't dreaming right now, and that this physical universe is not just a part of an elaborate dream? But Descartes didn't stop there. He further argued that perhaps there was an all-powerful evil-deceiver that was fooling us into believing that a physical universe existed. The only thing that escaped Descartes' arguments was the existence of his own mind, for if the evil deceiver was fooling *him* – then *he* must exist – hence his famous statement: "I think therefore I am." I love Woody Allen's version of the theory: "What if nothing exists and we're all in somebody's dream? Or what's worse, what if only that fat guy in the third row exists?" Still . . . Questions.

If a field of study is to be judged by the progress it has made, philosophy would not come out at the top of the class. The questions the pre-Socratics dealt with are the very same questions contemporary philosophers grapple with today. Questions such as: How was the world created? What is a soul? What is considered an ethical life? And, of course: Is there a God? Philosophers today are no closer to the answers to these questions than Thales was in 540 BC. But philosophy doesn't deal in answers, it deals in questions.

Don't misunderstand me. Philosophers offer answers to their myriads of questions. The answers tend to be long, complex, and often indecipherable. But a trained thinker can usually pull apart the answers. There are always counter-arguments, and then counters to the counter-arguments. But the questions . . . they are indisputable.

Philosophy wasn't always about questions, though. It started out as a field that offered solid answers. Before the advent of philosophy in ancient Greece, people utilized mythology to answer life's biggest questions. Stories about the gods and their battles were conceived in theater and literature. Marduk, the chief god of Babylonia, was born. Zeus and Apollo took center stage in Greece and Rome. The universe and its mysteries were explained away with the tales of the extraordinary lives of these divine beings. Philosophers were the first to take the magic out of the mysteries. They developed scientific theory. They observed nature and created rational rules to explain their observations. They were the first to place the mysteries of the universe under the domain of the human mind.

This was the type of philosophy that appealed to me as a young adult in university (which explains my focus on classical and medieval philosophy as opposed to modern thought); I loved the idea that life's big questions were within the purview of man's reason. I loved the notion that if I put my head to it, I could come up with solutions to the universe's most basic questions. In retrospect, I should have focused on the questions more than the answers, but who wants to contemplate evil deceivers when you can attain the answers to life's biggest questions? So, that is where my story really begins, with answers. It was the answers that were ultimately responsible for challenging my core beliefs and leading me down the bleak road of doubt. The questions just picked up where the answers left off. But I am getting ahead of myself.

I grew up in an unassuming brick home in Forest Hills, New York, with my parents and two older brothers. We lived down the block from the famous Forest Hills tennis stadium, where they used to play the U.S. Open. While we weren't tennis fans (never even went to a match), we did take advantage of our location. My brothers used to sell parking spots in our driveway during the big tennis games. They used to weave their ten speed bikes through the rows of cars on our street asking people if they were looking for a parking spot. I remember standing on the sidewalk watching and thinking: Why do they always get to do all the cool stuff? My mother got to join in the fun, too. She worked as the parking lot attendant (that master's degree in special education really came in handy, Mom). She spent her days moving cars around the driveway so that people could get out of their spots. My brothers still glow when they talk about their entrepreneurial days. Strangely, I don't get the sense that my mother recalls those days with the same fondness.

My home was a warm religious one, where faith in God was a given. Nobody needed to discuss it; God was the backdrop to our lives. We celebrated the Jewish holidays that marked miracles performed by God for the Jewish people. We lit the menorah on Chanukah to commemorate the Jewish victory in the time of the Hasmonean Temple. We dressed up in costumes on Purim to celebrate the Jewish victory over the wicked Haman. We made a *seder* on Passover to commemorate the escape of the Jews from Egypt. We marked Yom Kippur by fasting, because we believed that on that day God judged us and decided our fate. God was central to our lives; and the belief in Him was unquestioned. God symbolized security, meaning, love, and discipline.

There was a certain innocence that characterized my religious beliefs as a child. Judaism was the air I breathed, the water I drank, and the bread I ate; there was simply nothing else.

I vividly recall my first encounter with a different religion. It took place over a passionate debate about God with my two neighbors, Tami and Laura. We were sitting in front of Laura's house. Like my home, it was a reddish brick house with two small gardens on either side of its entrance. We sat on the brick staircase that led up to the front door discussing world religions, God, and all the other things six year olds are known to discuss.

"Cheryl, my mommy told me that my God and your God are the same God," Tami explained. Tami and I were both Jewish.

"That's right, Tami, we both believe in the same God," I proclaimed, proud to have her in my club.

"What about my God?" Laura chimed in.

"Well, who is your God?" I asked, happy to be the authority on this subject.

"My God is Jesus, our Lord and Savior," she answered.

"Oh." I puzzled over her response. I had honestly never heard of that God before. To be honest, I didn't even understand some of what she said.

"I don't know. I'll go ask my mom."

That night I had an eye-opening conversation with my mother.

The fact is that while my religious beliefs expanded and intensified as I grew older, they still retained a quality of innocence, and even a lack of sophistication. I studied the Bible in a religious day school where the day was broken up into morning religious studies and afternoon secular studies. I remained on this dual program throughout high school. I knew just as much about my religion as I did about math, science, and history. I was a good student, too. And religious subjects were often my favorite (with the exception of fourth grade . . . but that's for my next book). I was very content with my beliefs. I had never understood people who denied the existence of God. To me, God's existence was self-evident. The complexities of this perfectly integrated universe clearly attested to a God. Religion was the most reasonable option for me. I was completely unprepared for what was to come.

♦   ♦   ♦

I started university as an English major, mostly because it involved three of my favorite pastimes: reading, writing, and over-analyzing. After my first semester, however, I was disappointed with my English classes. Or, perhaps I should say, I was disappointed with myself. I found that I wasn't doing as well in my classes as I had expected. That was difficult for me because as a high school student I was at the top of my class, and English had been my favorite subject. It was hard enough going from the god-like existence of high school senior to the mouse-like status of college freshman. I wanted to excel again. A good friend suggested I try philosophy.

"Philosophy?" I asked. "What can I do as a philosophy major?" I was picturing myself on a street corner in a toga handing out flyers.

"Just try it," she pushed. "I promise you'll love it."

And I did. My first philosophy class was Ancient and Medieval Philosophy. I was hooked after day one. I finally found a field populated by people who over-analyze more than I do. But it was more than that. Philosophy felt like trying on a new sweater and finding that it fit perfectly; it felt comfortable, but new at the same time. I started the next semester as a philosophy major, and my long career of hyper-thinking things took on new proportions.

As a philosophy student, I was particularly drawn to the medieval period. The medieval philosophers were religious, like me, and often grappled with issues of faith and reason. Many of them believed that faith and reason walked hand-in-hand, and that reason did not contradict the basic tenets of faith. They developed philosophical arguments, which looked something like proofs for geometry problems, to prove the existence of God. I fell in love with these arguments; they confirmed my belief system. They confirmed that reason was a corollary to faith – not a challenge to it.

The arguments have big names – the Ontological Argument, the Cosmological Argument, and the Teleological Argument – but they are really rather simple. (Philosophers love to give multi-syllabic names to relatively simple concepts. It makes them sound smart.) A great formulation of the Teleological Argument, for example, comes from William Paley, an eighteenth-century thinker.

Paley posed a hypothetical situation. He said, suppose while walking, I kicked my foot against a rock, and was asked by an onlooker where the rock came from. It would not be unreasonable for me to suggest that the rock had always been there since the beginning of time. But suppose I encountered a watch in place of the rock. If asked about the origin of the watch, I could not suggest that it had been lying there for eternity. Why not? Well, clearly the watch was constructed for a purpose – to tell time. And clearly the watch was constructed from specific parts that perform specific functions.

The argument was fairly straightforward: Just as a watch, with its intricate construction and useful design, must have been produced by an intelligent designer, the universe, with its vastly more intricate and purposeful design, must have a designer. This type of argument for the existence of God has had several permutations both before Paley and after, but the basic reasoning was always similar in its simplicity and intuitive nature.

My initial attraction to medieval philosophy eventually turned into something only slightly short of an obsession. I studied the works of Maimonides, Gersonides, St. Anselm, Augustine, and Averroes. (I tended to be drawn to the medieval rationalists as opposed to the more mystical schools of thought.) It came to a point where I began to think like a medieval rationalist. Most people don't know this, but medieval rationalists thought differently. They banked it all on the human intellect. They believed that on some level, the human mind could reach God's, and unite with it.

Adopting Aristotelian metaphysics, they believed in a system of mediators between ourselves and God, who were called "Intellects." These Intellects governed the planets, and their job was to contemplate God. The final Intellect – the "Active Intellect" – controlled our world. By developing our own intellects to their greatest potential, we could unite with the Active Intellect, and receive enlightenment. This was the route to God; via our intellects we could on some level read the mind of God. This unfettered celebration of human reason characterizes medieval philosophy.

I bought into the system. Not the planets being governed by Intellects, of course. Once Galileo came around with his nifty telescope, much of Aristotelian philosophy was brought to its knees. But I was hooked on the intellect drug. I believed that my intellect was my direct route to God.

This had its consequences, you know. I became a closet intellectual elitist. I secretly believed (or, at least I hoped it was secret) that I was smarter than most, because I was a card-carrying member of the school of medieval rationalism. I tried not to let these beliefs slip into conversations with friends. They were mere mortals. They would never understand the secret code of the medieval intellect. I kept it close to my heart, and pretended to be as weak minded as everyone else. But inside, I knew.

There was, however, one aspect of medieval philosophy that troubled me: its conception of God. Medieval thinkers believed that God could not undergo change, such as emotion or movement. For them change implied imperfection. So they labeled God the 'Unmoved Mover': He made the world go around without moving or changing himself. God remained completely static in the philosophy of the Middle Ages.

This ultimately created problems for medieval religious philosophers like me. If God remained the same, how could He have knowledge of us? After all, we change. If God had intimate knowledge of all our various changes, then wouldn't the content of His knowledge change? And wouldn't that imply a change in God? And if God *didn't* have knowledge of people, where did that leave religion?

It was a brick wall for us medievals. Many fervently held on to the belief that God had knowledge of people. They claimed that the human mind is not capable of understanding God's knowledge; it defied all categories of human understanding. So yes, He did know us, and no, He still didn't change.

This solution was difficult for my highly developed medieval brain. It directly flew in the face of my superior intellect. After all, we super-intellects should have some insight into the way God works! That's what the whole system was built upon! I mulled over the problem for a while, and slowly, I became affected by it.

My iron intellect had been penetrated. More importantly, I would soon realize, my religious convictions had been challenged. I was slowly sinking into the quagmire of a religious crisis. But it was the philosophy of the eighteenth-century German philosopher, Immanuel Kant, that propelled me to the bottom.

◆　◆　◆

Immanuel Kant was born in 1724 in the city of Konigsberg, where he lived out his life. His parents were strict pietists, and he received a rigid religious education that emphasized religion over science and math. It always fascinates me that a man who started out life in this fashion would cause a revolution in philosophy, metaphysics, and ultimately, religion.

At the age of forty-five, Kant was appointed professor of logic and metaphysics at the University of Konigsberg. He spent the next ten years in isolation. Apparently, he was thinking. You have to respect a man who could do nothing but think for ten solid years. The fruit of his thought was his famous *Critique of Pure Reason*, an 800-page book of almost inaccessibly dry philosophy. It was difficult to understand, but when people finally figured out its meaning, it had unsurpassed influence in philosophical circles. It literally changed the way people thought about *thinking*.

In his *Critique*, Kant analyzed the medieval philosophical proofs for the existence of God. But after careful analysis, he concluded that the proofs fail. You see, Kant had set out to describe the limitations of the human mind. That should have been a red flag for me because, while we medieval thinkers acknowledged some limitations, we really put all our poker chips on the mind and its ability to reach God. Kant set out to prove that this was impossible given the limited confines of human reason.

Kant's theory of human knowledge is a bit complicated. According to Kant things can only be understood within the concepts of time and space. These two concepts are imprinted in our minds, and all data that our brains receive from our senses are then placed within these two structures of understanding. Think of the Yellow Pages. There are hundreds of thousands letters and numbers that go into the telephone book. They would all be completely unintelligible to us if they were not placed within certain classifications and categories. First we must organize the letters into words or names to allow them to express articulate ideas. Then we need to alphabetize the names and divide them into locations so that we can utilize the information for our needs. Similarly, we need to assign area codes to the phone numbers, and put them in their proper places. Once the letters, words, and numbers are placed within certain structures of understanding (grouped into words, alphabetized, and categorized by location) can we begin to understand the Yellow Pages. For

Kant the structures of understanding reality are time and space. We need to place things within time and space in order to understand anything.

But here's the thing: time and space only exist in our minds. Things that lie outside of our minds (i.e., reality itself) don't exist in time and space, so they cannot be apprehended by our intellects. So how can we know anything? Our senses provide our mind with data. The things in themselves appear to us in a certain way. We *see* a messy desk, we *hear* our children laughing, we *smell* our dinner burning. These sensory impressions get passed along to our minds and are then placed within those two all-important concepts: time and space and applied to certain categories (quantity, quality, relation, and modality). Only then do we begin to understand these things. But we can't understand them as they truly are. We can only understand them as our senses apprehend them. In short we can only know what our eyes see, and how our eyes see them. We cannot know the things in themselves. I can only know how my eyes perceive the messy desk; I can't know the actual desk. And equally important: things that cannot be grasped by our senses at all (things that cannot be seen, heard, smelled, tasted, or touched) cannot be processed by our minds.

But this is where the problem comes in. If our minds can only understand things it receives from our senses, and those things are only understood through the concepts of time and space, then our minds cannot prove the existence of God. God cannot be perceived by our eyes, ears, nose, mouth, or hands. And God cannot be understood through the concepts of time and space – He is beyond those realms. So God is strictly off-limits to our minds (as are all objects of metaphysics).

What I found most baffling (at the time), was that Kant goes on to claim: "I got rid of reason to make room for faith." Painstakingly severing the connection between faith and reason, he simultaneously claimed to have saved faith. (For Kant, belief in God is necessary for morality.) Although many people might have found this line of thought to be clever, even brilliant, to me it was unfathomable. To my rational mind it was impossible to conceive of faith without reason. Reason was supposed to be the most direct route to God, and now Kant claims that it can't even prove God exists?

Coupled with my medieval doubts of Divine knowledge of human affairs, the Kantian lack of rational clarity regarding the very existence of God sent me gasping for air. If my reason couldn't prove the existence of God, what could? A very painful battle was waged inside my head the year I was first exposed to Kant. The doctrinal beliefs of my childhood, the very glue that held my psyche together, were fighting against these seemingly heretical claims that I encountered as a philosophy student in college. Suddenly, everything was in doubt. I couldn't get it out of my mind.

Kant was everywhere. I sat down to make the proper blessing on my food, and Kant sat across from me. He was challenging me. Did I really know if there was a God out there listening to my blessing? And if there was, how was I to know if He cared?

Yom Kippur was a day of utter confusion A unique day on the Jewish calendar, Jews are told not to eat, drink, or even wash themselves; we are all ascetics on Yom Kippur. It is a day completely dedicated to our relationship with God. But the Yom Kippur after I met Immanuel Kant was dedicated to something entirely different: internal mayhem. There I stood in synagogue on the holiest day of the year, asking God for forgiveness, and in the same breath doubting His very existence. I was guilt ridden, but I wasn't quite sure why. Kant stood next to me in synagogue, with his starched white wig and devil-red overcoat, whispering harshly into my ear while I attempted to pray. "How can you be sure there is a God?" And I had no response. I was confused, and lost, and had been rendered mute. I was being haunted.

I looked over at the other worshipers. The men were wrapped in their prayer shawls, heads bent down towards their prayer books, completely un-aware of the presence of the eighteenth-century philosopher at my side. They were clearly oblivious to his arguments. Or perhaps they knew something I didn't know. The women next to me were equally devoting themselves to their prayers. At times a song would erupt from the cantor's mouth and the congre-gation would join in. The songs made it a little easier for me. I never noticed it before, but there is something about music that makes it easier to believe in God. I looked over at Immanuel Kant. Did he hear the music too?

It is difficult to describe what the very threat of a life without God felt like to me. I suppose it was something akin to a bee hive without its queen bee. Leo Tolstoy describes such a hive as follows:

In a queenless hive no life is left, though to a superficial glance it seems as much alive as other hives. The bees circle round a queenless hive in the hot beams of the midday sun as gaily as around the living hives; from a distance it smells of honey like the others, and bees fly in and out in the same way. But one has only to observe that hive to realize that there is no longer any life in it. The bees do not fly in the same way, the smell and the sound that meet the beekeeper are not the same . . . . Instead of a neatly glued floor, swept by the bees with the fanning of their wings, there is a floor littered with bits of wax, excrement, dying bees scarcely moving their legs, and dead ones that have not been cleared away. (*War and Peace*, Book 11, chap. 20)

This is what life had become for me. Outwardly, things didn't change much. I went to classes, took exams, wrote papers, and conversed with friends. There was no hint of an internal crisis. I had become quite good at hiding it. Even my four roommates, who were my closest friends, had no idea. It was a struggle to keep it from them. We talked about everything in that small dorm room on 34th Street in Manhattan. We discussed dating, school, life aspirations, and some less sublime things like, Why do you have to snore so loudly? And, Whose turn is it to clean the bathroom? It felt strange to keep something this big from them. But I wasn't confident in their ability to help me. Besides, I didn't want to ask my questions out loud. I didn't want to hear my voice say the words. I felt that once the words acquired an existence outside of my own head, they would somehow become more real. So I distanced myself from my friends emotionally and I began to live a double life. Nobody knew that my queen bee had died.

◆ ◆ ◆

This was my state of mind on that wet day in April. As I sat alone in the empty university cafeteria, with my neglected notebooks open in front of me, Kant's assertions were going through my head. I almost didn't notice my friend approaching me.

"Hi Cheryl! I haven't seen you in a while. Are you going back to the dorm now? Maybe we can walk together."

Lisa and I had been very close friends at one time, but, as with so many of my friendships, I had been neglecting ours of late. I had planned to go to the library after lunch to start a long-overdue paper, but when I looked down at my notebook, I couldn't even remember what subject I was supposed to be studying.

"Sure," I said. "Just let me pack up my lunch and I'll walk with you."

Leaving Kant behind, I packed up my things and prepared to leave.

That's the last thing I remember about that rainy spring day. Little did I know that would be the last day I was to be haunted by the ghost of Immanuel Kant.

CHAPTER TWO

Elihu's Tale

ELIHU WROTE FOR hours, stopping only here and there to locate a word or rephrase a sentence. When he finished, he surveyed his work. He was genuinely pleased by what he saw. It was a good beginning:

A man by the name of Job lived in the land of Uz. He was an honest, wholehearted individual, with a sincere fear of God. He was blessed with seven sons, three daughters, and a good deal of wealth. He was well-respected among his neighbors. As a devoutly religious individual, Job was very concerned with sin. So much so, that when his children would gather for a party, the next morning he would always bring sacrifices to God, lest his children had sinned at the party.

Elihu smiled to himself when he read over that portion of his tale. He had been thinking about a particular neighbor of his who was known to do that. This neighbor ended up losing his home, and was taken to exile with Elihu. But he never stopped believing in God. The exile had in fact made him even more devout. He was convinced that his sins caused him to lose his home. Who knew? thought Elihu. Maybe he was right. But maybe there was more to it. With that brief reflection, Elihu went on reviewing his work:

God had been consulting with his angels, when Satan arrived to join them.
"Where have you been?" God inquired of him.
"I have been roaming the land," Satan explained.
Satan had indeed been roaming the earth, performing his task. It was Satan's

job to reveal the true depths of a person. Satan himself was a firm believer in the notion that there were no genuinely good people in the world. Everyone had an Achilles' heel. The secret was how to find it. That was Satan's self-appointed task. He tried to locate that weak spot in every person that would lead to his moral and religious downfall.

"Have you noted my servant Job? Is there anyone more honest and genuinely afraid of sin than he?" asked God, perhaps a bit proudly.

"That's not surprising," answered Satan. "Look what you have given him. I wonder what would happen if you took away his wealth and his family."

God thought about it for a moment and replied, "That's an interesting point. Satan, I give you full reign over Job's possessions and children," Then He added, "Just don't touch his body."

Elihu paused again. This last passage had been excruciatingly difficult to write. He had to somehow convey that the fate of Job was ultimately in God's hands, but at the same time he didn't want to openly condemn God. The condemnation would come later, from the mouth of Job himself. Elihu was aware that he was walking a theological tightrope by introducing Satan as a protagonist, a kind of agent for God's shadow side, but he didn't want to give the end of the tale away before the debate started. And he knew his message had to come in the form of a debate. He knew his message was a process, not an answer. So Elihu chose to go with Satan for now. He took a deep breath and secretly hoped it wouldn't backfire:

The party was in full swing. The seven sons of Job set up a festive table complete with meat, olives, and wine. They invited their sisters to join them, and pretty soon the whole town came. That was when they heard the shouting.

"They took them! They took them all!"

Confused, the sons started to run toward the field, but the chief shepherd reached their party first.

"What happened?" they asked.

"A band of thieves stole the cattle! They took it all. It's all gone!"

That's when they smelled the burning grass. They saw a boy running toward them screaming, "Fire! Fire! The sheep! The sheep!" They shielded their faces from the oncoming smoke. It was blowing at them with such ferocity that they hardly noticed the windstorm that was responsible for the spreading smoke.

Within seconds they found themselves at the center of the storm. They ran for cover under the table, but the wind quickly robbed them of their refuge. The trees were rocking precariously. Dust, food, and vegetation swirled through the air, dancing violently with the storm. Finally, with one swift turn of the wind, the tornado took everyone with it.

Job had just finished offering his best animals up to God when he received word of the multiple tragedies. For that one brief moment, everything ceased. Not a blade of grass fluttered in the wind. Not a speck of dust swirled in the air. Job had seen the messenger's lips move, but couldn't hear a word of what he said. He was a solitary audience of a silent show. Then, like a stick catching ablaze, his entire being erupted. The messenger's words sank in, and Job's body folded to the ground. He tore at his clothes in desperate mourning, and proclaimed loud enough to convince his own soul, "God giveth, and God taketh away."

To Satan, it was an unimaginable response. But God, of course, could not be surprised. He observed these events and was satisfied with the results. He wasted no time pointing it out to Satan.

"With all due respect," Satan replied, "His body wasn't harmed. It was just his possessions and his children. What would happen if his own body was somehow damaged?"

Satan was becoming anxious. He had taken a bit of a gamble with Job, and Job was not cooperating.

"Okay," God responded, reluctantly agreeing to set His stakes higher.
"But don't kill him," He warned.

Elihu set his scroll aside. He had written enough for one day.

CHAPTER THREE

Creases in my Blanket

April 26, 1993, Bellevue Hospital

I AWAKE FROM MY dreamless state to find myself in an unfamiliar room. The room is dimly lit and has two rows of four to five beds. I am lying in one of the beds. The sheets are starched white and pulled tightly over the mattress. My blanket is pulled perfectly over my body without a crease. Each bed has a wooden nightstand next to it and a curtain to enclose its little niche. My mom sits at the foot of my bed with her knees folded up to at her chest, and her bare feet resting on a chair. She seems to be asleep.

"Mom?" I ask, "Where am I?"

"Huh?" she grunts.

I have clearly woken her up. Her bloodshot blue eyes pop open instantly as if they have been trying unsuccessfully to stay open for hours. At first she looks confused, but then it seems as if some very sad reality sets in, and she begins to focus on me. My mom, usually meticulously dressed and fully made up, looks markedly different. Her clothes are wrinkled from being slept in, and her short, thin, wavy reddish brown hair is mussed. Her face looks ghostly pale and her mouth is set in a half frown.

"Cheryl, are you okay?" she asks.

"I think so," I respond. "But where am I?"

"You don't remember?"

"Mom, what are you talking about? Where am I and why are you sitting with your knees at your chest?"

"You are at Bellevue Hospital," she responds. "I'm sitting like this because I saw a rat running around here," she adds, with disgust.

"The hospital?" I am confused. I have no memory of being brought to the hospital.

"You really don't remember?" she asks, as she slowly gets up, carefully checking the ground for scurrying rodents. She comes over to my bed, and while adjusting the blankets, continues, "You were hit by a car." She speaks slowly and deliberately as if she is explaining something to a three-year-old.

I try hard to remember the incident, but I feel an unrelenting pounding in my head.

"My head is killing me," I complain.

She nods. "That's from the accident." Her next words are delivered slowly. It's as if by measuring each one she could somehow shield me from the next.

"On your way to your dorm, a taxi driver lost control of his car and hit you. You were dragged by your knee and you hit your head on the pavement. They claim you don't have a concussion, but I don't know how that is possible."

She takes a deep breath and continues, "Cheryl, all the skin was torn off a large portion of your leg, and your kneecap was shattered."

I swallow hard and try to digest what I have just been told. I look down at my blanket covering my legs. I hesitate, and slowly lift it. My left leg is completely covered with hospital bandages. I sigh, relieved that I can't see what lies beneath the bandages under the blanket. My mother quickly tries to straighten out the creases in the blanket, as if by fixing the creases she could fix what's under them. I am beginning to understand that defeated look in her face.

"Will I have to have surgery?"

"Daddy and I are switching you into another hospital," she says, glancing at the rats scurrying in the corner of the room. "We just haven't picked one yet. We are looking for the right surgeon."

"Was anyone else hurt?" I ask, trying hard to get the full picture.

"You were walking with two friends. But they were only lightly hurt.

"What about the taxi driver?"

"He was brought to the emergency room to be treated for light scratches," my mom grimaces, clearly disgusted by the unfairness of the whole thing.

Due to the yet undiagnosed concussion, my once trustworthy mind wanders, as the rats scurry aimlessly about. I find it frustratingly difficult to focus, and the pressure in my head is unyielding.

"Try to get some sleep," my mother continues, while stroking my hair. "It's late."

I look around the room. There is one other occupant who lay fast asleep on her hospital bed.

"Why don't you go home and get some sleep in your own bed? At least you won't have to contend with the rats," I offer.

I am making a half-hearted attempt to assert my independence. It's funny how I have spent most of my early adult life rejecting her over-protectiveness, and now I am just glad she is there. Thankfully, and predictably, she replies, "No, I'll just sit here by your bed – in case you need anything during the night."

We look at each other knowingly. Perhaps she could protect me from the rats, but there was no way she could protect me from what lies beneath the creases in my blanket.

◆ ◆ ◆

The day after the accident I was transferred to Columbia Presbyterian Hospital. My ride to the hospital was a lesson in pain management. There were four of us in the ambulance: my mother, the driver, the paramedic, and me. Apparently I was not given adequate amounts of pain killer, and every bump in the road sent a searing pain up my leg which elicited a loud groan from me. I was beginning to make the other occupants of the ambulance nervous. Feeling like every groan was an indictment of the hospital, my mother complained, "Why didn't they give her more pain medication?"

The paramedic blushed and hastily returned to checking his machines and my IV. The driver of the ambulance was growing more and more frustrated with every groan.

"I'm trying as hard as I can!" He eventually shouted, and I immediately regretted my reaction to the pain.

"I'm really sorry," I said, meaning every word of it.

I promised myself I would try harder to hide my reactions. I started to try to rationalize myself out of my feelings of discomfort. It doesn't hurt that badly, I reasoned. It could be a lot worse. It's only a dull sensation. I focused on the roof and paid attention to the wail of the siren. I had never been in the back of an ambulance before. I pictured the other cars on the road moving over to the side of the street to let us by. They would probably be wondering who the patient was inside the ambulance. I had never been the answer to that question before. Controlling the pain is all about focus, I concluded as another flash of it shot up my leg. But we'd better get there soon, I thought, again and again.

We reached Columbia Presbyterian hospital, and I was brought to an examination room to meet my new doctors. My case was to be handled by two separate surgeons. Dr. Snider, a reconstructive surgeon, was to handle the skin graft, while Dr. Kaplan, an orthopedic surgeon, would repair my kneecap and torn tendons. The doctors were a study in dichotomy. Dr. Snider was of medium height with brown hair and a warm smile, while Dr. Kaplan was tall and thin with gray unkempt hair and huge eyes that seemed to pop out of his head. He reminded me a bit of Christopher Lloyd in the movie *Back to the Future*, and I must admit to having my doubts after meeting him for the first time. These doubts would later prove unfounded.

I was taken to my room – a standard hospital room replete with overpowering smells of various germ-killing agents. The walls were white, as were the floors, sheets, and pillowcases. The wooden door to the room sat on one side of the bed, and a thick colorless curtain hung on the other, dividing me and my sole roommate. She was a sweet elderly woman whom I dubbed "the woman behind the curtain" for obvious reasons. I never saw her, nor did I know her name; yet, she still remains one of the most vivid recollections of my hospital stay.

Our first conversation was a bit strained. Neither of us wanted to impose, but each of us was curious about the other. I heard her muffled cough and sudden cries, and asked, "Are you okay?"

"Yes. I'll be fine," she responded.

"Do you need anything?" I asked. "I could call for the nurse."

"No. That won't be necessary. I just had heart surgery, and I'm in pain. But they gave me a pillow to hug when the pain gets very bad."

A pillow? I thought, as I looked at my trusty morphine drip that they hooked me up to. I was connected to a state-of-the-art pain-killing machine that allowed me to control my own dose of morphine, and she was hugging a pillow. I couldn't believe she was downplaying her predicament. I heard her muffled cries and felt completely helpless. I had never heard an elderly person cry before. It was a sound I never want to hear again.

"Why are you here?" she asked, after recollecting herself.

"I was hit by a car," I explained.

"What happened to you?" She asked.

I felt silly complaining, but I responded, "The skin was torn off my leg. I'm going to have surgery in a few weeks."

"Oh!" I heard her say. "That must be quite painful."

I didn't know how to respond. I knew that in theory my injury was excruciatingly painful. Without skin, all the nerves were exposed. But my pain was so well controlled, that I literally felt nothing. I knew this was not the case for my roommate, and I didn't want to draw attention to that fact.

"It's not so bad," I muttered, and the conversation turned into an awkward silence. As I pushed the button on my morphine machine, I could hear another muffled cry. My heart broke with every groan.

As I lay silently contemplating her plight, I thought back to the ambulance ride. I remembered how difficult it had been to hide my pain, and it occurred to me that perhaps one measure of a person lies in the grace with which she accepts her pain.

◆ ◆ ◆

A day or so later, I was transferred to a private room. I knew that in theory this was considered a better alternative, but I missed having a roommate to take my mind off my own injury. The room was a small one. It had just enough space for my hospital bed, which was equipped with the requisite gray tray and overhanging television set. There was not much to do in a private room. My leg was immobilized, making movement nearly impossible. So I divided my time between watching soap operas and looking out the window. I can't remember the view I had, but I believe it involved the side of a building and a tree.

My hospital stay was a degrading experience. I couldn't get up from my bed, so I was unable to take care of my basic daily hygienic needs. Going to the bathroom and bathing became public events. Every morning a nurse came in to help me bathe, and bring me my bed pan. If I threw up from my medication, I had to summon the nurses to clean it up. If they were busy, I had to sit in my own vomit until they could come. I had become completely dependent. My self-esteem slowly dissipated into the heavy, uncontaminated hospital air. There were days I wished I could dissipate with it.

Visitors would come to try to cheer me up. My eldest brother lived close to the hospital and he often dropped in. My other brother was spending a year in Israel with his wife so he couldn't visit, but we spoke on the phone. One of my roommates came by a few times. She had a cheerful disposition in general, and she brought it up a notch or two when she visited. It didn't do much to cheer me up, but I appreciated her trying.

My parents were with me all day, every day, for the first two weeks. They came early in the morning bearing forced smiles and cards and gifts that people had sent with them. My mother was my interior decorator. She would plaster the walls with well-wishers' cards, and stuff the corners of the room with dolls. My favorite doll had been a soft white polar bear, whom I dubbed "Aristotle."

One day, after about two weeks, my mom came in with her usual stockpile of cards.

"Good morning, Cheryl! How was your night?"

"Okay, I guess."

"I brought you cards from a few of your friends," she said, showing me her pile.

"I'll look at them later," I responded.

Sighing, she nodded, and sat down next to me.

"Cheryl, if it's okay with you, I won't come to the hospital until the afternoon tomorrow."

"Why not?" I asked.

"Because there isn't much to do here, and I really do need to go back to teaching."

Had the sheets beneath me suddenly become rougher? My pillow harder? My blanket scratchier? I shuffled around uncomfortably.

"Okay." I finally agreed.

The next day was the first morning since the accident that I was to spend without my parents. I woke up with the sun, and looked around. There wasn't much to see, so I flipped on the TV. The morning shows had just come on. The actors bore their fake smiles well, but their cheerful chatter just grated on my nerves. I turned off the TV, and looked around again. My eyes fell on the phone. I reached for it, but then pulled back. I knew I shouldn't. I was twenty-one years old. I had been out of their house since I was seventeen, and I had woken up every day since then without them. So what was so different about today? I hesitated for another moment before I picked up the phone.

"Mom?" I said.

"Cheryl?" I heard on the other end. I had clearly woken her up. I could picture the concerned expression in her swollen tired eyes. I knew I shouldn't be doing this.

"What's wrong? Is everything okay?" She asked.

"Yeah," I responded.

"Do you need me to come now?" She asked.

"Yeah." I responded.

I'm still not quite sure how she sensed that from the first "yeah." But she was there in a half hour. I can't explain why I needed her. I just know that at that point in time, I couldn't remember a time that I didn't need her. My lack of independence was changing me.

But there were more troubles lurking. I discovered two of them one afternoon in the hospital while receiving a visitor. The visitor was a Rabbi from my university. He was a well-known Jewish activist. He was tall, silver-haired and had an important air about him. I would later find out that he had sat with my parents for hours while I was first brought into the emergency room. He sat down next to me, looking very serious, and tried to make small talk. I was a little nervous about impressing him, and I was determined to sound intelligent and well-informed. He asked me about my classes.

"Let's see," I responded, "I'm taking . . ." I couldn't complete my thought. For a moment, I tried hard to concentrate on my life before the accident.

What did I do? Who were my teachers? What subject was I most interested in? I couldn't remember a thing.

"I have no idea what I'm taking," I whispered, a little stunned by the admission. I became increasingly agitated. Why couldn't I remember my classes? Suddenly it hit me. I had very little memory of my life before the accident. I tried hard to concentrate, but all I got was that incessant pounding in my head.

The doctors had been so focused on the devastating leg injury that they really didn't pay much attention to the head injury. But once my memory loss had been disclosed, they informed me that they needed to assess my ability to read. They hastily located a paragraph and handed it to me. I looked down at the page, a little shakily, but determined to read the contents. What I saw confused me. I was able to recognize the letters, but I couldn't name them or their sounds. It was the same feeling you get when you meet someone you know, but you can't quite place them. It was as if the connection between my thoughts and my ability to name them or express them had been severed.

The crushing leg injury easily overshadowed the head injury. But it was the head injury that left me bereft of my ability to remember, to concentrate, to read, and to think on a sophisticated level. I had a vague notion of what I enjoyed reading prior to the accident. I knew I was attracted to the Jewish philosopher Maimonides, and the German philosopher Immanuel Kant. But I couldn't remember what they said, or why I was drawn to them.

I knew that I had been a philosophy student, but I couldn't remember what a philosophy student does. I had misplaced my tools, so I was out of a job. And like any newly unemployed person, I was lost.

◆ ◆ ◆

I will never forget the day I encountered my new knee.

The day started off well enough. My parents arrived that morning unusually hopeful. After three long weeks in the hospital, covered by bandages, my knee was about to make its first appearance. I could sense the nervous anticipation from the doctors. This was a particularly large skin graft, and they weren't one hundred percent sure that it "took." If it hadn't, I was told, I would need another surgery. I was unsure of what they meant by "took." I assumed it meant that my knee should look pretty much like it did before the accident.

The intern was the first doctor to arrive that morning. He was young and energetic, and clearly excited by the prospect of unveiling his masterpiece. He confided to me that he had been allowed to take part in the operation. I understood from his comment that this had been his first operation. I wasn't quite sure how I felt about being his science experiment, but I didn't have much time to harp on it.

One by one, the other doctors appeared. My parents were asked to leave the room, and I got a funny sense that had the knee not been connected to my body, I too would have been asked to leave. This was the doctors' show, and I was just along for the ride.

The surgeon slowly peeled away the bandages. There were quite a few layers, and it took some time. Finally the bandages were set aside, and my knee was exposed. I peeked over the surgeon's head, and immediately regretted it. I could hear the doctors congratulating themselves on a job well done. Apparently, the graft "took."

"Wait a minute," I heard myself saying, "You mean this is good? This is what it is *supposed to* look like?"

The knee was covered by four distinct sections of braided raw skin that clung tightly to the bone beneath it. It wasn't uniform in color – it was varying shades of pinkish/red, and it was stapled to my leg with large silver staples. It was fair to say that it looked *nothing* like my knee prior to the accident.

"It's going to look better, right?" I interrupted the doctors' conversation. "I mean, when it heals."

The surgeon looked at me blankly, and responded, "It won't look as raw, and we will remove the staples, but other than that, this is pretty much the way it will look."

I swallowed hard. Why hadn't anyone warned me? I had just assumed that my knee would be restored to its natural appearance. I didn't quite know what to make of it. I needed time to figure out a way to accept the fact that my leg was . . . disfigured. My mind was reeling and I could only vaguely make out what the doctors were saying. They seemed to be analyzing each section of the graft, and finally they covered it with new bandages. I was glad I didn't have to look at it anymore. I needed time to acclimate. The orthopedists would come and cast my leg the following day. Without looking back, the doctors left the room. As far as they were concerned, their job was done. As far as I was concerned, maybe they could have done it a little bit better.

◆　◆　◆

Three and a half weeks after I was hit by the car, I was due to return home. I was excited to leave the hospital. The hospital was a world completely set apart from the outside. It functioned on its own rules. It had its own dress code. It had its own smell. It had its own population. But it was more than that. The hospital reminded me of my disfigurement. It reminded me of bedpans. It reminded me of IVs. It reminded me of disease. It reminded me of dependency. It reminded me of morphine and the way the elderly lady in the next bed cried. It was, as far as I was concerned, a prison; leaving would be my emancipation.

I was not in a physical state to go back to university. I still had no memory of my classes, I was unable to read, and I was encapsulated in a full-leg fiberglass cast. So when I left the hospital, I went back to my parents' house.

When I hobbled through the door I was expecting to see the familiar home I grew up in. But something had changed. I couldn't put my finger on it at first, but something felt different. Had my parents changed something in the house? Was it the color of the walls? The floors? The furniture? I remembered that when I was a child my mother used to surprise us when we came home from summer camp, with new wall paper, or carpeting in our rooms. But the walls and floors were the same. So what was different? And then I passed a mirror, and saw my reflection for the first time in three and a half weeks. Had it only been twenty-four days? My cheeks had once been round and small, now they were long and thin. I used to have freckles sprinkled across my nose and cheeks. They had completely vanished. My eyes that had once been steel blue were now a slate gray – almost not a color at all. My hair had once been shoulder-length and coiled. Now it hung past my shoulders like a water-logged washcloth. All at once, I knew what had changed – it was me.

CHAPTER FOUR

Revealing and Concealing

BACK IN MY old home, I slowly began to re-discover myself. I had taken on a different persona in the hospital. I was completely passive. I was a victim. I had lost my independence and my self esteem. But it only took a couple of weeks for me to get back into the swing of my old life. Being in my childhood room, with my old sweatshirts, and my box of Entenmann's cheese topped buns, helped me to remember what it was like to be me. My mom's rich chicken soup helped me get my body back up to speed. My face became round once again, and some freckles started to mamba around my nose and cheeks. Most important of all, I rediscovered my sense of humor.

Strangely, it was my crutches that reintroduced me to laughter. The crutches were pure fun for me. They allowed me to get around easily, and after weeks of being bedridden in the hospital, I greeted my freedom of movement like a slave who is suddenly liberated. Stairs, however, were an issue for me. I was taught by the occupational therapist in the hospital to go down stairs one at a time, placing the crutch down first, bending the good knee and putting the injured leg down next. But the process of going up and down became entirely too cumbersome. I was convinced I could halve the time using my method. It was really quite simple. I placed the crutches down on the step below, swung my body over them, and landed on both feet another step down. I was becoming quite good at it too, until the day my parents' friends came to visit.

They were sitting downstairs in the living room talking in hushed voices, and when I peeked over the banister, I could see that they looked very serious. I knew that I was the topic of conversation, so I decided to show off my new method. I thought it might lighten up the room a bit.

Okay, here it goes, I thought. I placed the crutch on the first step, swung my body, and landed perfectly on the second step. See? That wasn't too hard. Again. Place the crutches. Swing the body. Land. Again.

Now I was coming into full view of the spectators below. I smiled to myself, knowing that they were impressed with my method. Place the crutches. Swing. Uh-Oh.

Before I knew it, I had swung too far, and I was falling face first down the staircase.

"Ahhh!" I screamed, in panic.

My dad had been leaning against a wall at the base of the stairs. He hastily looked up at the sound of my cry and spotted me torpedoing toward him. I can still recall his facial expression in detail; His bulging eyes desperately trying to comprehend what was about to happen, his mouth straining to create intelligible sound, his fiery scarlet skin violently clashing with the peach carpeting that covered the stairs.

"Ahhh!" he eventually managed to scream.

"Ahhh!!!" the spectators joined in.

My dad held up his arms, and I landed – hard – into his chest. We were both a bit stupefied at first. I knew that I had survived the car accident, but would I outlive my new method? I did, but I don't think my dad was ever the same again. Needless to say, I abandoned my method. It needed tweaking.

◆ ◆ ◆

There were two phases to my recovery. Phase one involved recovery from the physical trauma; phase two involved recovery from the intellectual one.

Five weeks after I returned from the hospital, I had an appointment at the orthopedic clinic at Columbia Presbyterian. I arrived in timely fashion, and made my way over to the crowded waiting room. The surgeon was scheduled to remove my cast. I had been conflicted about this appointment all week. On the one hand, the removal of the cast marked my re-entrance into independent life. I would soon be able to shower independently, walk unencumbered, and go up and down stairs at will. On the other hand, the removal of the cast meant that I had to once again encounter my disfigured leg.

I was soon shown to a curtained off area, where I met my orthopedic surgeon.

"Sit down over there," Dr. Kaplan instructed, pointing to the examination table behind the curtain.

I hobbled over to the table, placed my crutches on the side, and ever so carefully slid myself onto the table.

"Here?" I asked, always unsure of myself.

He ignored the question, and picked up the largest looking chain-saw-type machine I had ever seen.

"You aren't going to use that on my knee?!" I asked.

He ignored the remark, and powered it up.

"You do know what you are doing?" I asked, quickly reviewing his qualifications in my head.

He smirked, and started to cut away at the only layer of protection I had against my new knee.

When the cast was completely removed, he carefully examined the knee. It had some degree of motion, and he was clearly satisfied. I glanced at it, careful not to take in the whole thing at once. I would only get that one quick glance, because the doctor covered it with an Ace bandage after his examination. He showed me how to wrap it tightly, to give my knee support, but not too tightly, to prevent cutting off circulation. This was a process I was to repeat often, as I would need to readjust it throughout the day. I was relieved that my knee wasn't exposed, and I carefully hopped off the table, grabbed my crutches, and hobbled out of the clinic before the doctor had a chance to change his mind about covering the knee with the Ace bandage.

As it turned out, the daily bandaging was a cathartic process. I'd wake up in the morning, and be forced to face my injury. As I re-wrapped the bandage, I studied the knee. I became familiar with all its ridges, cliffs, and mountain ranges. I knew where the shades of red skin merged into the shades of peach. I followed the changes in texture, as the smooth areas gave way to rougher ones. I slowly revealed the knee to myself, as I concealed it from others. Often during the day, I found myself on the floor removing the bandages and re-wrapping my knee, forcing myself to befriend it. By the time I was able to walk without the Ace bandage, I had begun to make a cold peace with my physical injury.

Once the cast was removed, I was able to start physical therapy. I didn't know how long the therapy would take because I was told that it depended on how committed I was to it. I had no idea that I was looking at months, not weeks. At first, things were strained between myself and my therapist. I didn't know what to expect, and I was wary of showing another person my leg. But after the first few sessions we became good friends. She showed me how to massage my graft skin to loosen it up and give it more flexibility. She taught me how to exercise my stiff kneecap. And when I was ready, she gave me leg strengthening exercises. I didn't notice it as it was happening, but I was slowly becoming less self conscious about my leg.

Then I showed it others.

It happened a few weeks into my physical therapy. I was sitting on the peach U-shaped sofa in my parents' living room surrounded by family members. My brother and his wife had recently returned from Israel and they were eager to catch up on things.

"Cheryl, how's your recovery going? Is the physical therapy difficult?" My sister-in-law asked. We had known each other since we were teenagers and we had always been very close.

"It's going well. The PT is tough, but I can walk now without a cane." I responded. I noticed my brother standing uncomfortably next to his wife. He hesitated briefly before he (inevitably) asked the question.

"Can we see it?"

"See what?" I asked stupidly.

"Your knee."

I didn't know what to say. I had never shown it to anyone but my parents and my medical team. I also felt uncomfortable about lifting my skirt. Religious Jewish women traditionally cover their legs (at least until directly past their knees) in front of men, and, depending on the family, this can also include siblings.

"I can't show you my knee! I responded, trying to laugh it off.

But they pushed and I had become somewhat acclimated to the unusual appearance of the graft skin and the way that it hugged my knee. Besides, I had managed to convince myself that it didn't look all that bad.

"Okay," I assented

I lifted my skirt slightly to reveal part of my knee. The room was enveloped in a stifling silence. I looked at my brother's face. He looked like he had just developed an uncomfortable rash. I glanced over at my sister-in-law. She looked just as uneasy. I looked down at my knee, trying to see what they saw. And I saw it. I quickly covered my knee, and joked, "It's not that bad, is it?"

"It's pretty bad," my brother admitted despite himself.

I hadn't expected that reaction from them. Clearly, the appearance of my leg (and they only saw a small portion of it) completely caught them off guard. They had a difficult time *pretending* that it wasn't awful. I learned something very important that day on the couch in my mother's living room: to myself I can reveal. To others, I can only conceal.

◆   ◆   ◆

Phase two of my recovery involved reclaiming my ability to read. As time went on, I had become frustrated and bored with the everyday tribulations of my physical recovery. I spent most of my days on the floor doing the leg exercises I had been instructed to do five times a day. When I wasn't stretching and lifting, I was walking around my parents' house in circles, a mouse on a spinning wheel. There was simply nothing to do. I didn't think I could read yet, so I couldn't study for my finals. The dean of my university decided that I wouldn't have to lose my whole semester of credits if I could successfully complete my finals. But how could I study if I couldn't read? The truth was that I had put off trying to read since the incident in the hospital because I was terrified to face that aspect of my injury. But at some point, I admitted to myself that I desperately missed reading. I didn't miss reading Robert Ludlum, or even Jane Austen. I missed reading philosophy. Philosophy had become an obsession of mine again. I craved it like I craved double fudge ice-cream. I missed the way it went down my throat – cold and indifferent at first, but then warm and familiar once it was digested.

The doctors couldn't predict when my ability to read would return. I would just have to try it out periodically. And one day, about a month after I returned home from the hospital, I finally hit pay dirt.

I entered my brother's old room, and sat at his wooden sailor desk. I picked up the book I intended to read. It was Kant's *Critique of Pure Reason*. I had no idea why I was drawn to this particular work. I opened it, and concentrated intently on the first words.

"H-u-m-a-n r-e-a-s-o-n," I sounded out each letter slowly . . . painfully . . . carefully.

I did it! I started to match more sounds to the letters. My head was pounding like a race horse in the final leg of a race. My brain was working so hard, I could almost feel it pulsating, connecting, functioning. I squeezed out some more words:

> *Human reason has this peculiar fate that in one species of its knowledge it is burdened by questions, which . . . it is not able to ignore, but which . . . it is also not able to answer.*

The reading was painstakingly slow, but after about an hour I completed a paragraph. My head was hurting and I had no idea what I had read, but I managed to read!! I went downstairs to share the good news with my parents. They were as delighted as I was. I was back on track.

From my perspective, at the time, the paragraph might as well have been written in Mandarin. I had no concept of its meaning. Later it would prove to be one of the most critical pieces in the puzzle I was about to construct in my mind.

CHAPTER FIVE

Elihu's Tale, Continued

SATAN SET TO *work. He wanted to come up with something good. He needed to strike the final blow that would incite Job to question God. He needed the cherry on his proverbial cake. He had already taken Job's possessions and children, now he would bring it even closer to home. And he had just the right thing for the task . . .*

Job was sitting next to his wife in ashes and thinking back to the times he had spent with his children. He remembered the first time he had taken his oldest – and at the time his only – son out to the fields. He showed him how to sort and dry the sheep before shearing. He explained that it was wise not to feed the sheep before they were sheared. Job remembered his son's tiny hands caressing the baby lamb. His hand was softer than the youngest sheep skin. He heard his wife speak.

"Remember when little Sara was born?" she asked, smiling wistfully. "After seven sons, God finally gave us a rosy little girl. I will never forget the way you looked when you held her for the first time. I think you were scared you would break her."

Job looked over at his wife. She had tears streaming down her face. She looked like a window in a rainstorm; She was completely transparent except for her tears.

He thought back to the birth of his first daughter. It was a spring shower on a hot, dry day: unexpected, refreshing, sheer joy. He remembered her as a toddler sitting on his lap and playing with his bushy beard. She had her mother's soft eyes.

That's when his skin started to burn. He rubbed his hand, but the burning wouldn't let up. Frustrated, he looked down, and was shocked to find that he had broken out in boils. His wife looked over at him to find out why Job was suddenly mumbling to himself and scratching, and almost fainted at the sight of the pus-filled red boils on his skin.

Then she felt the strangest urge to laugh. It wasn't a humorous laugh; it was the kind of laugh that keeps you from crying yourself to death. She emitted this odd sound, turned to her husband and demanded, "When will you finally take God to task for what he's done to us?"

Job didn't answer at first. Then he muttered something about taking the good with the bad, and sat quietly brooding. But inside, he was beginning to wonder about God . . .

CHAPTER SIX

Setting my Caterpillar Free

THE EIGHTEENTH-CENTURY FRENCH writer, Voltaire, once said, "Judge others by their questions rather than by their answers." Questions come in two varieties. The first type flow naturally. You might be listening to a lecture or talking to a friend, and you hear something puzzling so you ask a question. Often you don't have much invested in these questions. They serve to satisfy your intellectual curiosity, or some other practical function. But other questions fester. They lounge and grow more potent, wine in the barrel of your mind, until the time comes to bring them up from the cellar and uncork them. It often takes an event or an emotional trigger to bring out these questions, but once they're out, they can never be shelved again. These are the type of questions that alter your life.

My question started innocently enough. A little over a week after I returned home from the hospital, I ventured out to a friend's wedding. This was a big outing for me. I wasn't very mobile yet and I hadn't seen many of my friends since the accident. I was eager to get back into the rhythms of normal life. But I'm not sure I was ready for what I was to encounter.

I was seated next to one of my college roommates. The room was extravagantly decorated with huge chandeliers, maroon carpeting, and elegant tables. My leg rested on a felt chair next to me. The cast was up to my thigh, making sitting an uncomfortable proposition. It struck me that my leg had acquired its own persona, requiring its own chair, like the others at the table. It sat there reflecting a shadow on the floor, a dead tree blocking out the sun. When the music started to play, everyone made a mad dash to dance. At traditional Jewish weddings, when the bride and groom walk into the room (at least half an hour after everyone else is seated) they are mobbed by the celebrants and carried like soccer heroes out to the dance floor.

I sat alone at the table, with my fully-cast leg resting on a chair. The music was loud and obnoxiously happy. The women at my table shrieked when my friend, the bride, entered the room. She was quickly whisked away by the jubilant dancers, a princess with her courtly maidens. I stroked my cold fiberglass cast and thought that this should have been the most exciting time of my life, too. But I sat alone, with my leg, at a table.

That's when it happened. The question that had lingered in my subconscious, a caterpillar in its cocoon, waiting for the day I would set it free. I don't remember what did it. Perhaps the music, or the dancers, or the sheer jubilation of the wedding participants that set me apart, a storm cloud on a bright summer day. Something at that wedding set my caterpillar free because I found myself asking THE question:

Why did God do this to me?

It came upon me silently at first, like a soft tap on the shoulder, but it slowly grew in strength. I found myself trying to shake it off, reason it out. But the more I reasoned the larger it grew. The question seemed to take on a life of its own and it eventually set off an explosion in my brain that defied all proportions. WHY DID GOD DO THIS TO ME?

I racked my brain to recall the events of my life that led up this accident; but to no avail. My memory of my life immediately prior to the accident was still incomplete, however I was convinced that I hadn't done anything evil enough to warrant this degree of punishment. The fact was, as far as I could remember, I was a pretty good person prior to this calamity. I had been kind to an extreme. I had studied the Torah fervently. I was a solid friend and a loyal daughter. The question had grown a proportionally. Soon it completely overpowered me. I needed some answers.

PART TWO

CHAPTER SEVEN

Elihu's Tale, Continued

ELIHU RETURNED TO his tent after a long day. He desperately needed some rest, but his mind kept returning to the conversation he had overheard that afternoon. He had been tending to his olive stand when he heard a commotion coming from the far end of the marketplace. He ran to the crowd to see what was going on. The prophet Ezekiel was addressing the people. He looked tired and his voice was hoarse, barely audible, and yet his message was loud and clear:

"You relied on the strength of your swords. But it didn't get you far! You have soiled the Holy Land with your sins and God has forced you out. You should know by now that it was your own abominations that forced you out of the Holy Land!"

The vendors and shoppers began to grumble. Many of them clearly didn't agree, and even more simply couldn't care less. But that didn't stop Ezekiel from prophesying. Elihu remembered a conversation he once had with Ezekiel in which the prophet described his Divine visions as something akin to a sudden, overwhelming urge to sneeze; he couldn't hold it in if he tried.

"God does not want the evil man to die. What good is his death to God? God wants him to return to righteousness and repent from his evil ways."

The crowd started to disperse. Many simply wrote Ezekiel off as another nutcase in the marketplace. But there was one group of men who were having a heated debate over what they just heard. Elihu recognized these three individuals as Levites who used to serve in the Temple. The oldest of the group covered his face with his aging hands and cried, "Oh, if they would only listen! Don't they see their own sins have caused this tragedy?"

The second Levite hastily agreed. "How could they be so blind? They are raising their children to follow in the ways of the pagans. Their children have been our downfall!"

But the third member of the group couldn't disagree more. His face was gray as the evening sky, and his arms hung low at his sides as if they were being pulled down by some unknown force. "What do their sins have to do with me? Have I sinned? Why should I suffer this exile? Why did my home get destroyed? Why have my children been killed?" As he mouthed the last words, his voice started to crack. He knew his children were innocent victims of the war. They saw the Temple burning and they ran to protect the holy vessels. But in the end, they were turned to ash by the flames of the Holy Temple. They were his final sacrifice to the God he was no longer convinced even cared.

Elihu wanted to jump in and defend God, but he couldn't find the words. Perhaps if he went back to his manuscript! He knew that once he started to write, the words would somehow come . . .

◆ ◆ ◆

The *Book of Job* has always been a mystery to me. Its authorship is unknown, and the Rabbis have attributed it to just about every major time period in Jewish history. Was it written during the time of Abraham? Moses? The destruction of the Temple? The fact is, it doesn't matter. It could potentially describe anyone from any time period. It is a story of the human condition. A righteous individual loses his wealth, family, and his health for no apparent reason. It is a scenario that most of us have encountered more than once in literature, art, and, unfortunately, also in life.

And while my suffering couldn't begin to compare to Job's suffering, or to what many other people have to endure for that matter, I somehow felt connected to Job's plight. The question of bad things happening to good people is seemingly unanswerable. But the beauty of the book does not lie in its poetic inaccessibility. The *Book of Job* is an invitation to a debate. Job is not simply expected to accept his fate; he is applauded for challenging it. And, like a rare Picasso canvas, the *Book of Job* is the subject of intense scrutiny and commentary. Kant notwithstanding, my journey really began with the *Book of Job*.

• • •

Job was sitting on the ground examining one of his boils when he heard the sound of hooves pounding on the dirt. He looked up and saw his three good friends: Elifaz, Bildad, and Tzofar coming up the road to visit him. They had heard about his difficulties and they had come to extend their condolences and comfort. Job heard the youngest of the three, Tzofar, hop down from his donkey and walk over to help Elifaz, the oldest of the group. Slowly the three inched forward to greet Job. At first, they said nothing. What could they say? Every time someone thought of something, he'd re-think it and discover that it wasn't enough . . . Finally Job spoke.

"I curse the day I was born," he exclaimed. "And the night I was conceived."

Elifaz opened his mouth to respond. His beard was a mixture of gray and white, and his eyes were the color of the bark of the old oak tree that he would sit under to read religious and mystical texts. His shaky hands bore the marks of a difficult life.

"You have suffered much, Job. But we all must agree that there is no man without sin."

Job couldn't believe what he was hearing. He had lived his life as a righteous man. What sins could he possibly have committed to warrant this type of punishment? Was Elifaz implying that his sins caused these travesties?! No, it wasn't anything he had done that caused this. And that's what he told his friends.

"Perhaps you haven't sinned, but your sons must have." His second friend, Bildad, blurted out.

Bildad was middle-aged, and not quite as learned as Elifaz. But he had access to certain traditional texts, and he made use of them.

"And if they didn't sin, surely they will receive recompense in the World-To-Come."

His words did not appease Job. In fact, Job became infuriated.

"God does not care for man," he claimed. "He doesn't even know man." Tzophar, the youngest of the three, couldn't hold back any longer. "What do you

know of God?" he asked. "God is not controlled by human wisdom. He is simply controlled by His will. We have no right to question God's will," the young man exclaimed, becoming more fervent by the moment. His face matched his flaming red hair, and as he finished speaking, he took a long drink of water.

What would happen, Elihu wondered, pausing for a moment to massage his aching quill-hand, if I were to stick myself, blatantly, into this book? How would readers relate to me as a character? Let's find out.

The four friends continued to debate. Tensions were high among them. They had been arguing all day, and the sun had nearly completed its descent into the horizon, when they heard the sound of a man clearing his throat. They hadn't noticed the young man standing in the back of the tent. His hair was the color of the sand, and his eyes were the color of the clear sea in the springtime. His name was Elihu, Hebrew for "He is my God." Elihu was just past his teen years, younger than the other four men, and thus reluctant to disturb their conversation. But the conversation was taking such drastic turns that he felt it would be in everyone's interest to hear what he had to say.

"Will you excuse me?" he asked politely. His voice was soft, that of a shy child, but at the same time steady, that of a man who knew what he was talking about.

"Job, I have listened to your views concerning God and His governance of this world, and I respectfully disagree. God knows people. God communicates with people. Sometimes He communicates in a dream. Sometimes He communicates through a sickness. The point is to see your sufferings as a type of communication with God. Perhaps, He is trying to tell you something . . ."

Job didn't have much time to consider Elihu's words. He felt a strong wind at the entrance of the tent. Securing his robe tightly around his waist, he rose to close the flap. As he reached the opening, he peaked out of the tent to locate the source of the wind. And there, by the ghostly glow of moon, he encountered God.

CHAPTER EIGHT

Neither They Nor Their Reward

THE ABUNDANCE OF commentaries on the *Book of Job* left me slightly bewildered. Where should I start? After brief reflection, I decided to start at the beginning: with Saadya. Rabbi Saadya Gaon (882–942) was the first major Jewish philosopher, and a paradox of sorts. He was the leader of the Jews in Babylonia, and a man of strong principles – rare for a politician of his caliber. The Jews of Babylonia in the tenth century were ruled by two political bodies: The Exilarch – the secular ruler who interfaced with the non-Jewish authorities – and the Gaon, the community's spiritual leader. In 928, Saadya was appointed Gaon, and it only took a couple of years for his principles to cause him to come head-to-head with the Exilarch, a man by the name of David Ben Zakkai. They quarreled over an inheritance case that was decided by Ben Zakkai, which Saadya refused to endorse. The Exilarch summarily put a ban on Saadya, and appointed a new Gaon. Not to be outdone, Saadya outlawed Ben Zakkai and appointed a new Exilarch in his place.

It was petty politics served up with a religious twist. Saadya stood up for his principles; in this case, it was what he believed to be religious law. Saadya was eventually removed from his position of power for five years. During those years he wrote prolifically, and, ultimately the beneficiary of the whole dispute is humanity, for we now have the first major work of Jewish Philosophy, entitled *The Book of Beliefs and Opinions*.

David Ben Zakkai wasn't the only one who challenged Saadya's principles. You see, one of the latter's most fervent principles was the absolute justice of God – a fact that was disputed, inter alia, by none other than Job. Saadya needed to come up with a solution that would restore equity in the universe in light of the suffering that befell people like Job.

He explained that righteous people suffered for one of two reasons: Either they were being punished for some small inequity, or they were being tested by God. Why would an omniscient God need to test people? God tested people either to increase their reward in the World to Come, or to showcase the righteousness of the person in question. God only tested those He knew could pass, due to the public nature of these tests. Job's test fell under the latter category. Job was tested in order to demonstrate to the world that he was worthy of all the blessings he received. In his commentary to Job, Saadya explicated this theory further.

He explained that the angels in the story of Job weren't heavenly beings. They were people – Job's neighbors. Satan was also a person. He was one of the neighbors. He was called Satan because he was an adversary of Job's. This group of people, led by Satan, challenged the worthiness of Job. They slandered him and claimed that he did not deserve what he had. Thus, God contrived this test to prove Job's worthiness to Satan.

Saadya's analysis continues with an obvious question: What about children who suffer? Surely a child couldn't commit a sin that would warrant excessive suffering. And is it fair to test a child? And what about the innocent children of Job who seem to be pawns in this trial contrived by God to test their father? Saadya claimed that a child suffering is like a father instituting corporal punishment, or like a bitter medicine that a child must take so that in the end, the child will benefit.

Clearly, there were big problems with this solution (certainly to the modern ear) but I decided to focus on what was right about it before I figured out why it bothered me so much. Saadya was part of a philosophical school of thought called the Mu'tazilites. The Mu'tazilites were staunch defenders of Divine Justice. According to this school of thought, Divine Justice is similar to human justice. A standard model of human justice would dictate that evil gets punished and righteousness gets rewarded. The Mu'tazilites understood

God's justice as functioning along a similar paradigm: if man sins, he pays the consequences. If man is good, he reaps the rewards.

On the other hand, the Asharites, an opposing philosophic school of thought at the time, didn't believe we could hold God up to our standard of justice. God functions on a completely different plane – He defines His own concept of justice. To the Asharites, God could cause righteous people to suffer, and evil people to succeed, and we would still have no right to question Him. It clearly just falls under God's conception of justice. It doesn't have to fit human categories.

This is Saadya's frame of reference, and it explains his solution. His staunch belief in the accessible nature of Divine Justice is the backbone of his theory. This is a concept that I supported, even if the implications for the innocent were on the draconian side. After all, without this basic premise in place, where would my search for the reasons behind my accident lead? I would be faced with the Asharite response: God decided that this was His will, so don't ask questions.

The Asharite version had some serious problems. Firstly, it left me feeling jilted by God and not knowing why. In my view, a good solution would have to perform two functions: it would have to be rational, and it would have to provide some sense of closure. With the Asharite theory, I would have walked away bitter and unresolved.

The second problem with the Asharite version of things was that it led to some perplexing questions. If God's concept of justice and man's concept of justice are two completely different things, what is the source of man's concept of justice, and how do we know it is indeed just? And is there any possibility of making sense out of this universe? One wonders what kind of God would create a race that is completely incapable of making sense out of its own existence. Are we all just victims of a completely inexplicable fate? It is a terrifying thought, and more relevant to me, one that is not supported by the Torah, which has been the guiding philosophical force in my life since I was old enough to speak.

The Torah is replete with examples of Divine Justice; God warns us to follow His commandments, and promises us recompense. Similarly, God warns us against defying Him, and promises to punish those who don't comply.

Justice from the Torah is completely understandable and functions within the confines of human justice. This important concept is what Saadya wished to defend with his solution to the problem of righteous people suffering.

But Saadya's solution obviously has its problems too, even for those of us who have taken the leap of faith in the Torah as a Divine work. When I first read it, I couldn't help but wonder if Saadya's world wasn't just too black and white. He assumes that no matter what type of pain you were afflicted with, there was a just reward that would eventually make it all worthwhile. But what about Jewish suffering during the Holocaust? What about the father forced to watch his hungry child slowly fade away? What about the mother who for sixty years can't escape the image of her terrified child being beaten and killed by an inhuman soldier? Can any amount of reward make up for Nazi Germany? There are some types of suffering that just don't seem worth it, no matter what the reward.

It seemed to me that Saadya put so much emphasis on the World-to-Come that he neglected the reality of this world, and the need for some sort of justice here and now. And you can't help but think that an omnipotent God would be able to provide some sort of equity in our world too.

The Talmud relates an interesting story, or Aggada, to illustrate this point. The story involves Rabbi Yochanan, who lived in the third century in Palestine. Rabbi Yochanan was unusually handsome and immensely popular, but his life was riddled with hardship. His mother died in childbirth, and his father had died soon after he was conceived. He had ten sons of his own, all of whom died during his lifetime. He was said to have carried the tooth of his youngest child around with him to help console others. Apparently, he was aware that no matter what state of suffering a person was in, they would be consoled by the fact that they weren't living with what Rabbi Yochanan had to live with.

The Talmud relates that once Rabbi Hiyya bar Abba fell ill. Rabbi Yochanan came to visit him, saw him in his weakened state and asked, "Are your sufferings welcome to you?" Rabbi Hiyya bar Abba replied, "Neither they nor their reward." Rabbi Yochanan responded by asking for the hand of Rabbi Hiyya. Rabbi Hiyya yielded his hand and was uplifted by Rabbi Yochanan and recovered.

One day not too long after that incident, Rabbi Yochanan was ill. Rabbi

Hanina came to visit him, and asked, "Are your sufferings welcome to you?" Rabbi Yochanan responded, "Neither they nor their reward." Rabbi Hanina asked for Rabbi Yochanan's hand, uplifted him, and cured him.

Rabbi Eleazar fell ill next, and Rabbi Yochanan came to visit him. He found Rabbi Eleazar weeping, and after some inquiry discovered that Rabbi Eleazar wept because he contemplated death. Rabbi Yochanan agreed that this was a cause for crying, and they both wept. Rabbi Yochanan asked for the hand of Rabbi Eleazar, uplifted him, and cured him.

It is an intriguing story. Doubtless, there are many interpretations for this piece of Talmud, as there are many unusual points to contemplate. Firstly, why were the Rabbis grabbing hold of each other's hands and how did that heal them? Secondly, why did Rabbi Yochanan need Rabbi Hanina? Couldn't he heal himself as he had healed the others? Thirdly, what was their view of reward and punishment?

Think back to the last time you had a cold. Remember the dizziness and pounding in your head? Remember the feeling that if you closed your mouth you would suffocate because there was no virtually no air coming in and out of your nose? Remember visiting the doctor and silently praying that you had bacterial pneumonia or some other horrible (but curable) infection, anything but a cold? Pneumonia meant a prescription and some sympathy. At least you wouldn't get that condescending, cold-hearted response from your doctor: "It's just a cold."

There is only one thing that works to ease the burden of the simple head cold – a hand. When a visitor comes and listens to you complain, holds your hand, and empathizes with your plight, suddenly you feel a little better. There is a commandment in the Torah to visit the sick. The Torah recognizes the healing quality of a hand, or an ear. Rabbi Yochanan, who had lived a life of suffering, understood this from his own experiences. That's why he couldn't do it for himself, but he could do it for others.

The issue of the Talmud's response to reward and suffering is a bit more complicated. We can understand their rejection of suffering, but who in their right mind would reject the reward?

It is my feeling that the Rabbis weren't rejecting the reward. They were rejecting the reward as an answer to their suffering. The Rabbis recognized the fact that while we do receive reward, it cannot explain away the problems of the righteous suffering. Rabbi Eleazar went a step further. He is said to have been crying over the final fate of man. It is a puzzling response considering the Jewish belief in an afterlife. Especially in light of the fact that the afterlife in Judaism is one in which man reaps all of his spiritual rewards. So why is death worth crying over? Rabbi Eleazar was testifying to the fact that those rewards are indeed wonderful, but they couldn't console people over their ultimate demise. Death is still a frightful fate, despite the rewards. Rewards were like dessert after a meal of three-day-old, overcooked, dried out leftovers; they were sublime, but they didn't necessarily make the meal worth eating. I was with the Rabbis on this: I had big questions about dessert.

◆　◆　◆

Saadya's discussion of ultimate reward made me think back to a certain incident that occurred approximately two months after the accident. It was time to address the insurance issue. My father had a policy with his car insurance company that covered me in case of car accidents. It was up to me to prove to them that my injury was substantial enough for them to pay out the full value of the policy. My father hired a friend of his to be my attorney. Don was a tall man with a thick head of black hair and a nasal voice. He was a mild-mannered fellow with a desire to make things right. I'll never forget the first time he saw my knee. My father sat at the dining room table with him and discussed the details of the case. I was the unseen, silent member of the conversation. At one point Don looked up and said,

"I'm going to have to see it."

"See what?" I asked stupidly.

"I need to see the knee, so that I know what I'm talking about."

I didn't want to show it to him. I was still trying to come to terms with it, and I preferred to keep it to myself. Besides, I didn't like the way people looked at me after they saw it. I was taken aback by the request, and I didn't know how to respond. I looked to my father for help, but none was forthcoming. So I forced myself to lift my skirt.

He didn't flinch.

"I don't think we will have a problem getting what we are asking for," he said turning toward my father. I was the elephant in the room again.

It got worse. I was told that I would need pictures of my knee for the insurance company. My lawyer knew an appropriate photographer, and I was to meet my lawyer at the photographer's studio.

I met Don in front of the photographer's building in the midst of a busy street. I liked the everyday tone of the setting. It was public. It was crowded. For a brief moment, I allowed myself to imagine that I was there for another reason: To go shopping, perhaps, or to catch a movie. I didn't want to think of the image of my knee imprinted on a paper and passed among gawking strangers.

We walked into the photographer's studio, and I looked around. It was a standard studio, big enough to be a one-bedroom apartment, but it had no internal walls, so it was just a large room. It was almost bare, save the camera equipment scattered all over the floor. The carpeting was thin, the lights were dim, and a couple of backdrops stood in the center of the room. But something about the scenario felt very wrong. Photography studios were meant for photographing toddlers on rocking horses or teenagers for high school yearbooks, not disfigurements. "Stand over there," the photographer instructed. I have no recollection of what he looked like. He had no face. He was everyone. Everyone to whom I would be forced to display my knee. I stood beside an umbrella while he adjusted the lights. It was all so odd. Should I fix my hair? Should I smile? I was standing in front of a camera exposing something I had sworn to hide. I was exposing my soul.

SNAP.

SNAP.

SNAP.

I had no idea how many pictures he took. I thanked him quietly and left. I had never felt so naked in my life.

That wasn't the end. Three days later, my attorney informed me that the insurance company wanted to see the injury before a final decision could be made. I had to show my knee to more people.

My attorney picked me up at 10:00 AM to take me to the insurance company. We tried to make light conversation on the way. It went something like this:

"Hi Cheryl. How are you doing today?"

"Okay, I guess."

Silence.

I felt nauseous. After a thirty-minute car ride, we reached our destination. It was an attractive building on Long Island. When we reached the office, we were told to go into the conference room and wait.

The conference room was small. It was just large enough to house a cherry wood table and brown fabric chairs. I stood with my attorney near the table for a few awkward minutes.

"Cheryl, I don't know if I need to say this, but when they come in, don't smile and look cheerful," my attorney advised.

Look cheerful?! I thought to myself. It's hard to look cheerful while you're trying to keep yourself from throwing up.

The door opened, and a man and a woman walked in. They were clearly uncomfortable. After a few preliminary remarks, which I couldn't hear over the buzzing in my head, one of them said,

"Can we see the knee now?"

I think I stopped breathing when I unveiled my knee. I felt like I was on exhibit at a freak show. I don't remember when my breathing started again.

The insurance people looked even more uncomfortable than I was. They nodded, asked me a few questions about the surgery, and walked out. My attorney was satisfied.

A few days later, I found out that the insurance company agreed to give me the entire sum I had requested. I couldn't have cared less.

CHAPTER NINE

Lemon Bundt Cakes and Intellectual Freedom

HISTORICALLY, HUMAN SUFFERING has incited many staunch believers into questioning their faith in God. The Greek philosopher Epicurus, who lived from 341 BC to 270 BC, was credited with being the first to put forth the philosophical problem of evil with what came to be known as Epicurus's paradox:

> "Is [God] willing to prevent evil, but not able? Then he is not omnipotent. Is he able, but not willing? Then he is malevolent. Is he both able and willing? Then whence cometh evil? Is he neither able nor willing? Then why call him God?"

Epicurus was not a fan of religion. He often emphasized the destruction wreaked by organized religions – and I suppose on that point, he was correct. For Epicurus the gods existed, but they were material beings, who were composed of a substance that was continually replenished, thus making them immortal. These immortal beings, however, were not even aware of our existence.

In retrospect, I could have sided with Epicurus and ultimately denied that God had anything to do with this accident. After all, this accident was clearly an "evil." If God was all-good and all-powerful, how could He have caused the accident? Perhaps, philosophically speaking, I was not on purely rational ground when I chose to focus on why God did this to me. Yet, for some reason, and against all logical arguments to the contrary, I intuited that God had directly caused, or at least agreed to, this accident. It was a thought that I could not get out of my head, and I decided to go with it. Now it was my job to understand it, and I decided to pull out the big guns.

I turned to the greatest Jewish medieval philosopher, Moses Maimonides, who lived from 1138–1204. Before the accident, Maimonides had been my personal hero, because he fully espoused the principles of the medieval intellect (as I had). In other words, the primary task of his philosophy was to reconcile faith with reason. For Maimonides, reason came in the guise of Greek philosophy, especially Aristotle. He wrote *The Guide to the Perplexed*, in which he attempted to show that whatever reason had proven beyond a doubt was the true Torah view. Any seeming conflicts between reason and Torah implied a misunderstanding of the Torah.

Maimonides's philosophy book was no simple volume. He did not mean for just anyone to be privy to its contents. The weak-minded masses could not be trusted to have any inkling as to what was written in his book. How, then, does one write a book that is both accessible to those who need it, and inaccessible to those who won't understand it properly?

Maimonides came up with a brilliant solution. His book was essentially a 600-page puzzle. Chapters were out of order, and the book was replete with contradictions – all carefully placed by its well-intentioned author. That way, in theory, only the intellectuals could get at the book's real meaning. The downside is: *nobody* really knows the true opinions of its author. Intellectuals and average readers alike argue over the basic question: what is the puzzle, and what is the point?

The result is a plethora of commentaries – some so way off base that they are humorous. When I was in college, I managed to dig up a Freudian interpretation of the book. A pretty impressive feat for Maimonides, considering Freud was born in 1865 – approximately 700 years after the Passover eve in Cordoba, Spain when Maimonides came into this world.

What the elitist professors were unaware of was that I was the true holder of the key to understanding Maimonides. One needed to be an authentic medieval philosopher, as I was, to unravel the puzzle of Maimonides's mind.

Maimonides's philosophy was not the only thing that endeared him to me. His life was riddled with setbacks, religious persecution, and the death of loved ones. As a youth, state-sponsored anti-Semitism forced Maimonides and his family to flee their home in Spain. The Almohads had given the Jews of Spain the options of conversion or exile. To be forced to surrender your religious convictions meant abandoning your parents, your grandparents, your values, your beliefs, and your identity. Fleeing was the only viable option for many.

But a life on the run was unpleasant. Maimonides and his family traveled extensively, seeking security, and a place where they could peacefully practice their faith. First they reached Fez, Morocco, but a few years later, they were forced to leave there, as well. They traveled to Israel, moving from place to place, until they were compelled once again to depart. They finally made their home in Fostat, Egypt. Worn from their years of travel, they were eager for stability. With the death of their father, Maimonides's younger brother took over the family business to support the family. He dealt in precious stones, and he managed to support everyone for eight years. But Maimonides was not meant to live serenely.

After those eight quiet years, he received news that his brother's ship sunk in the Indian Ocean. At that point, Maimonides went into a deep depression. He was bedridden for an entire year. Maimonides was no stranger to suffering. I thought it would be interesting to see how he responded to Epicurus's paradox.

How could God cause evil? According to Maimonides, God doesn't cause evil for the simple reason that evil does not exist, and thus can not be caused by anyone. Things like a lemon-bundt cake, or a custard cream pie (forgive me, I missed lunch) are caused. Somebody had to make them because they are THINGS – delicious ones. One might even bite into the custard cream pie and ask the question – who made this? But evil is different. Evil is like darkness. When one walks into a room to go to bed, and flicks off the light, does he "make" darkness? Would someone enter the room and ask – who made this darkness? It is not a question that you would likely hear. I could talk about who makes light. I might mention GE or Thomas Edison (if I were in a sixth-grade play). But who makes darkness? I couldn't ask that question because darkness is not a thing – it is the lack of a thing. Darkness is – quite simply – the lack of light.

Similarly, evil is not a thing; it is quite simply the lack of good. Nobody can make a "lack" of something. Some use the analogy of a doughnut to explain this argument, and, being fond of pastry (as you now know), I am eager to expound on this allegory. The baker clearly makes the delicious sugary doughy part of the doughnut, but who makes the hole? It is a silly question. Clearly nobody makes the hole; it is simply a byproduct of the doughnut. It is simply the lack of the delicious sugary doughy part. You cannot directly cause a lack of something else, as one causes light bulbs, lemon bundt cake, and the sugary doughy parts of doughnuts. Evil is the hole in a powdered doughnut. It is not a thing; it is the lack of a thing. So, you cannot directly cause evil. God comes out of this argument smelling of lemon bundt cakes and powdered doughnuts.

The argument was popular in medieval philosophy. It was also espoused by St. Augustine and Thomas Aquinas. It stemmed from a neo-Platonic view of the universe in which the universe was a series of Godly emanations. Each emanation was less concentrated in Divinity, until it reached evil at the bottom of the ladder, which was quite simply the complete lack of Divinity. In all probability, Maimonides identified this lack of Divinity (or "privation" in medieval lingo) with Satan. There is disagreement among commentators about who Satan was for Maimonides, but the most convincing argument in my opinion is that Satan was privation. It was this privation of Divinity that caused evil and suffering to befall Job.

It was an interesting argument, but when I read it, I felt an indistinct chill in the room. I think it was coming from the book. It is difficult enough to be forced to live with suffering, but to be forced to deny its existence seemed cruel, not to mention unrealistic. I thought of my friend who had lost her baby a short time ago. Externally, she was brave and accepting, but I could only imagine what her internal life had been like. To carry a life inside you, fall in love with it, hold it closer to you than any other human being, to feel him kicking, playing, sucking his thumb inside of you, to spend your entire waking hour daydreaming about his tiny fingers and toes, and then to lose it all in one fell swoop ... she must have felt like an amputee losing a part of her own body. Her pain was real; it was not simply a lack of happiness. Her suffering was real; it was not simply a lack of joy. To suggest otherwise was insulting.

But as I reflected further on Maimonides's arguments, I remembered a funeral I had attended, for the mother of a close friend. The funeral chapel was decorated sparsely. It had ten to fifteen rows of wooden benches, and a wooden podium up front. The walls were bare, save one verse from the book of Psalms imprinted in gold on the wall closest to the podium. The funeral was very well attended. The benches filled quickly, leaving most of the crowd standing in the back. I didn't mind standing. Somehow it felt right to stand at a funeral. I felt like I was attributing honor to the deceased, a woman who had lived her life virtuously.

As I stood listening to the speakers, trying to hide the fact that at any given moment I could burst into tears, I began to reflect on the sadness of death . . . . Why are people so saddened by it? Certainly in a case where the deceased had lived a full life, leaving behind children and grandchildren to uphold her memory, there was no reason to be saddened by death. Especially for a religious family, who believe in the notion of an afterlife. But not one person in the chapel on that sunny afternoon could escape that thick feeling in his chest, that burning sensation in his eye, or the urge to sniffle. Why? Why is sadness involved in death?

The answer was fairly obvious, to anyone other than me, who was still living almost entirely in her mind. We are sad because this lovely woman is no more. We are saddened because we will never see her again, feel the warmth of her embrace, or smell the faint scent of her facial soap. We are saddened by the lack of this woman.

Slowly, things started to fall into place. Maimonides was not being cold-hearted when he described suffering as a lack of a thing. We suffer from the lack of a thing all of the time. Starving people suffer from lack of food. Sick people suffer from lack of health. Neglected children suffer from lack of love. Family members at this funeral were suffering from the lack of their mother, just as my friend suffered from the lack of her unborn child. Their suffering was not nullified by simply calling it what it was – a lack of something special. Often it is the lack of something that people suffer from the most.

69

I thought further about this funeral. It wasn't often that people came to-gether to celebrate the life of a person. Award ceremonies celebrate work, birthdays celebrate birth, anniversaries celebrate marriage, but what celebrates the full breadth of a person's life? Their funeral. His infectious uneven smile, her terrible diet, or her way of hugging you so tightly that you'd feel light-headed afterward. These are the things which make up a person, and our memories of him or her, and they only get celebrated when that person is no longer there to hear it. Perhaps *that* is the saddest thing of all.

I wonder if we need the lack of X in order to get us to appreciate it. Perhaps this was the sin of Adam and Eve. They had it all in the Garden of Eden, but were unable to appreciate any of it until they'd tasted from the tree of good and evil. They needed that tinge of evil to taste the good – like that obligatory pinch of salt necessary to bring out the sticky sweetness of a cinnamon bun (yes, I'm back to pastry.) Perhaps it is the very lack of something that allows us to experience something else more fully . . . but that didn't make the absence of it any less bitter. It was an interesting paradox, one which Maimonides perhaps intuited when he came up with his theory. If that was the case, I could not wholly disagree with identifying evil with privation.

But the second part of Maimonides's argument was something I still found difficult to accept. Maimonides concluded from the fact that evil was iden-tical to privation that God could not cause it, because a privation couldn't be caused. Privation *could* be caused, I thought to myself. Death might be a privation of life, but when someone died in a car accident, usually somebody was to blame for that death. Somebody caused it – despite the semantics. And the relatives had the right to inquire of God why He allowed it to happen. It seemed to me that that was one of the messages of the *Book of Job.*

◆　◆　◆

The semester following my car accident, I returned to university with one more semester to complete in order to graduate. I would be graduating with a BA in Philosophy as well as a BA in Jewish Studies. I was never confident around people who I felt knew more than I did. I had a knack for harping on what I thought to be my own intellectual inadequacies. The only exception was philosophy class. In philosophy class, I soared. I asked questions, posited answers, bantered with the professors, joked with the other students . . . I had found my niche. But after the accident, that all changed.

I remembered the feel of the cold stone floor beneath me, and the smooth plaster wall behind me, as I sat on the floor in the hallway the first day of the semester after my accident, waiting for my philosophy class to begin. It was a class in eschatology (End of Days) and I was looking forward to getting back on the horse, so to speak. I sat and waited and watched the other young women saunter into the room. But something was wrong. I no longer felt that wave of confidence. I no longer felt that tinge of superiority. I stumbled into the room and found a seat at the far side by the windows. The professor, a tall thin man with a sarcastic sense of humor, whom I knew well, didn't even glance at me. I started to sweat. I furiously rubbed my knee. Something was wrong. This was supposed to be my room. This was supposed to be my subject. But I was a stranger to everyone, including myself.

There was an outspoken Australian in the class whom the professor was obviously acquainted with. She was taking control of the class. She was taking my role. I just sat there and listened like everyone else. When the class was over, I packed up my things and walked out. The rest of the semester played out in much the same way.

The car accident had changed me in ways that I had yet to discover. My confidence was severely diminished. I felt strangely vulnerable. I remembered – before the accident – the feeling that nothing bad would ever happen to me. Unfortunate things happened to people in newspapers, or Sunday night TV-movies. *I* had been somehow immune to car accidents and degrading hospital stays. The accident had taken my invincibility away. Suddenly I was alone, exposed and utterly defenseless. I've read again and again that this is perhaps *the* salient, common, and enduring affliction shared by the victims of accidents and other traumas: The loss of your imagined immunity to life's hardships packs an everlasting wallop.

This new-found sense of vulnerability sent me scurrying into corners when others approached, like a frightened rodent. Only I didn't have a neat little mouse hole to protect me. So I sat scrunched up in desks on the far side of classrooms, secretly hoping nobody would notice me. The new Cheryl lacked presence. The new Cheryl lacked self-assurance. The new Cheryl lacked her niche. The new Cheryl could more easily be characterized by what she lacked than by what she had.

I had *become* privation.

CHAPTER TEN

Intellectual Nirvana

IN ANOTHER CHAPTER of his *Guide*, Maimonides gives us a second analysis of the problem of evil. He classifies all the evils of the world into three groups: The first category of evil befalls man because he is composed of a physical body. The human body is not immortal. It is subject to disease and deformity, by definition. The second category of evil is moral in nature. These are evils that man inflicts on others. The third category is evil that man inflicts upon himself. This last category of evil encompasses most of the world's evils, according to Maimonides. Man develops bad habits (too many baked goods?), and, as a result, he suffers. Ultimately, we cause our own downfalls because of our physical bodies, or our flawed relationships with one another, or out of our own folly.

Maimonides had a good point. When one thinks of some of the worst evils perpetrated by man, one might think of the Holocaust, or the World Trade Center bombings. Undeniably, these were all perpetrated by man and not by God. (Sometimes crimes are perpetrated in the name of God, but these are clearly distortions of the words of God, not a fulfillment of them.)

But then one looks at pictures of victims of these crimes – Holocaust survivors, with their skin pasted to their bones like dead wet leaves on a sidewalk, each one branded with the mark of their loved ones' killers; the families of the victims of 9/11, children who will never learn to ride their bikes with dad, mothers who will never again see the dimples on their daughters' faces when they laugh. And it is hard to accept the "man is responsible for evil" theory as the whole answer. All of these horrendous crimes were indeed committed by man. But what of God? Didn't He stand aside and allow these crimes to be committed? Wasn't His task to protect the innocent?

While my suffering cannot be compared to the victims of the Holocaust or 9-11, I briefly reflected on my own situation. I thought of the taxi driver who hit me. I didn't know much about him. I had heard that he was brought to the same emergency room to be treated for cuts and minor bruises. I had also been told that he didn't even inquire after me; he just walked out of the hospital when he was finished being treated. Did he feel guilty? Did he lie awake at night wondering if I had survived his mistake? Did he think: Maybe I was driving too fast? Or: I should have braked earlier? Or: I shouldn't have been thinking about my money troubles while driving?

Or perhaps he completely absolved himself. It was raining, and the car skidded, end of story. I had no clue. I never met him. But it was almost irrelevant. Even if he had committed some driving errors, or even if he was a horrible human being, why did God allow *me* to get hurt? Wasn't I an innocent bystander? Setting the responsibility squarely on human shoulders wasn't working for me.

Which brought me to more questions for Maimonides, this time regarding his third category – evils which man inflicts on himself. I wondered what the statistics were on diseases caused by a lifetime of bad habits. Heart attacks. Diabetes. Alcoholism. But what about the diseases that *aren't* caused by man? What about the random diseases? What about a baby born with Spina Bifida? What about a child living with cancer? These cannot be traced to man's folly. What was God's role in these scenarios? I wondered if Maimonides had been satisfied by these answers as he lay, completely bedridden from depression, after the death of his brother. It seemed to me that God's role in these situations was still unclear. I couldn't help but feel that Maimonides had either missed something, or was glossing something over.

Maybe Maimonides sensed the difficulties with his treatment of the problem of evil, because his work continues with yet another study of the issue. This time he analyzes the *Book of Job*. He begins his discussion by describing

Job as a morally pious individual who had acquired a popular conception of the meaning of happiness. For Job at the beginning of the book, happiness consisted of wealth, health, and children. It was only after he lost them that he was forced to encounter a new reality. God gave him a hint when he declared that man cannot know or understand His ways. Job grasped this, and the new reality dawned on him. For the first time, he started to conceive of happiness in a new light. Riches, children, and other forms of physical pleasure became secondary. Ultimately, it was knowledge and contemplation of God that replaced these physical joys.

Man could spend his life in contemplation of God. It was a level that Maimonides describes as having been attained by Abraham and by Moses. It was a level that was characterized by living in a completely separate realm intellectually, even while acting out life in a physical world. Man would continuously contemplate God while he was shopping, eating, and playing with his children. In this way one could achieve immunity from suffering. Man would no longer value the physical world, so when things went very wrong he would take it in stride. As long as he could continue to contemplate God, man would be happy.

Medieval philosophers identified this stage as that of the Acquired Intellect. Buddhists have a similar state: Nirvana. Victor Frankl, a Holocaust survivor who later became a prominent psychiatrist, described another type of immunity to suffering in his book *Man's Search for Meaning*. He writes:

> We who lived in the concentration camps can remember the men who walked through the huts comforting others, giving away their last piece of bread. They may be few in number, but they offer sufficient proof that everything can be taken away from a man but one thing: the last of the human freedoms – to choose one's attitude in any given set of circumstances, to choose one's own way.

Frankl describes his inner experiences in the concentration camps in the most surreal terms. He claims that while the physical and mental lives of the prisoners were devastating, many of their inner lives were deepened. Frankl describes one particular day in the camps when, in the midst of his freezing early morning march to the work site, the man next to him whispered, "If our wives could see us now! I do hope they are better off in their camps and don't know what is happening to us." The slightest suggestion of his wife transported Victor Frankl to another place. He began to imagine the conversation he would be having with her. She stood before him smiling and giving him encouragement. At that moment, he grasped the message that poetry and literature attempt to impart: "The salvation of man is through love and in love." From then on, writes Frankl, his wife became his escape. His body would be subject to intense labor in sub-human conditions, but his mind would soar.

One day while he was working in a trench, Frankl describes an overwhelming feeling of being able to reach out and touch his beloved wife. He could physically feel her; she was there. And then, in that brief other-worldly moment, a bird landed on top of a heap in front of him and looked him steadily in the eye.

Whether it is Maimonides's intellectual immunity, Buddhism's spiritual immunity, or Frankl's emotional immunity, becoming immune to one's suffering seems to be a distinctly human trait. Only people can overcome their own pain by simply thinking themselves out of it. I thought of the woman in the bed next to mine at the hospital. I had admired her resilience to the pain. She seemed to accept it and was willing to work through it.

But Maimonides was describing something different. He was talking about reaching a stage where you would hardly feel pain, because your mind is engaged wholly on God. It involves intense religious and intellectual training. It is a level that I couldn't imagine attaining. Even Maimonides conceded that a person would need a certain disposition, and have certain intellectual qualities, to achieve this level. Thus, as a solution it only partially worked. It was like an Olympic Gold medal; for the outstanding individual it was something to strive for, but for the average guy, it was inspiring, but irrelevant.

CHAPTER ELEVEN

Revealer of Profundities

DESPITE THE FLAWS in their solutions, Saadya's reward system and Maimonides's privation theory provided valuable clues toward the answers I sought. But I needed to dig further. So, I turned to Gersonides. Gersonides was arguably the most important philosopher after Maimonides. He was also an astronomer, mathematician, and inventor of mathematical instruments. He invented a special type of stick which he called the "revealer of profundities" to measure the distance between the stars. I was hoping he would reveal a few profundities to me when I opened his philosophy book, *Wars of the Lord*.

But my encounter with Gersonides turned into something much more significant. It turned into my re-introduction to the elite medieval mind. Gersonides's theory of suffering was an outgrowth of his theory of Divine Providence, and it was that aspect of the medieval mind that instigated my spiral toward religious skepticism so many months prior. My car accident had wiped out the weeks and months immediately before it, when I had doubted God's existence. I had forgotten the many nights of lost sleep, headaches, and depression that the guilt and the feeling of deep loss had caused. I had forgotten that I had reverted to a dark and terrifying place in my own mind, a deeply disturbing corner that I could not claw my way out of. I had forgotten the moments before my fateful walk down 34th Street, when I sat in the cafeteria wondering, but not wanting to wonder, if there was a God. And now, all that came back.

Gersonides's book was the polar opposite of Maimonides's *Guide to the Perplexed,* stylistically speaking. Maimonides wrote in riddles; Gersonides wrote logically and methodically, straightforward. He presented all the opinions of a certain philosophical topic, his criticisms of those positions, and then his personal theory. It was all so neatly laid out, it reminded me of my childhood home. Everything was in its place – ad nauseam. Later, in graduate school, I would diagram his arguments. You could make perfect squares out of them. They were flawless in their sheer orderliness. But they were disturbing, too.

After his death, Gersonides's ideas were labeled heresies by some. One thinker went so far as to dub the book *Wars Against the Lord.* Fortunately for Gersonides, his Biblical and Talmudic commentaries ensured him a place among the great rabbis of Judaism. But it was his philosophy that was my focus.

Gersonides adopted Aristotle's view of God. In Aristotelian philosophy, God was essentially a Super-Mind who contained no plurality and did not undergo change. God was perpetually involved in contemplating Himself, and knew nothing else. God could only know the universal laws that made up His own mind. These were the laws that ultimately controlled our universe, and in God's mind they were unified into one highly theoretical rule of nature. Thus, God knew the general rule of the game but He did not know the players – the people. Man had a route to God's mind via the intermediacy of the Active Intellect.

The Active Intellect was the intellect (a lesser mind) that directly controlled our world. It received its information from a higher intellect, which in turn received its information from an even higher intellect, and so on. But ultimately, it was God Who controlled the chain by emanating ideas to the intellects. The catch was that God did not know He was doing this. The whole system was mechanical. The ideas that made up God's mind overflowed onto the next intellect automatically, like a waterfall. These concepts sound strange to the modern ear, but they were widely accepted in the ancient and medieval world.

The trick for the medieval religious philosophers (Christian, Moslem, and Jewish alike) was to explain key religious concepts like prophecy, providence, and miracles in light of this view of God. Some rejected the system. Others tried to work within it. Gersonides accepted the system to a greater extent than almost any other major Jewish philosopher. He claimed that the universe was the beneficiary of general providence. This meant that God was aware of the general rules that controlled the world. But what about individuals? Did God watch over them?

Individual providence could only be earned, Gersonides explained. When one developed his intellect, he essentially plugged into the stream of thoughts emitted by the Active Intellect, and would thus be able to "read" the ideas contained in it. A man could figure out ways to avoid harm in this way. It certainly wasn't religion 101. There was no intention in this scenario, no warmth, no love. God did not know me; I just hooked into His mind.

So what about suffering? What caused righteous people to suffer if they were "hooked into" the Active Intellect? Gersonides explained that righteous people suffered during the moments that they faltered. Everyone faltered. If a righteous person sinned or even briefly thought of something that he shouldn't have, he disconnected himself from the flow of the Active Intellect. Thus, he suffered.

As strange as it might sound, Gersonides's theory spoke to me. You see, one thing that had always bothered me about the accident was that I didn't "sense it" coming. I woke up that morning like every other morning. I put on my shirt, skirt, and shoes like every other morning. Skipped breakfast and went to class – like every other morning. But why didn't I feel it? Why didn't I somehow know that today something would happen? I had always believed that if something terrible were going to happen to me, I'd "sense it."

I remember the day my grandmother died. I was thirteen years old. I was coming home from a long day at school thinking about nothing in particular. I walked steadily along the tree-lined street, but when I reached my house, something felt wrong. I crept up the stairs to the front door. I'll never forget the way the door looked that day. The white door with the black trim and the gold knocker looked ominous. I had no idea why but my heart skipped a few beats before I opened the door. There, on the silky peach couch, sat my mother's best friends looking uncomfortable, as if they had something to say but they weren't quite sure what.

"What's going on?" I asked, already almost hysterical by that point, for no reason I could name.

"Your mom is upstairs." One of them answered.

I ran up the stairs and found my mother, swollen-eyed and clearly trying to compose herself. She was a flower that had just lost its stem – vulnerable, abandoned, without a source.

"Cheryl, I have something very sad to tell you."

I can still hear her voice saying the words.

"Grandma died today."

I was very close to my grandmother. I was her only granddaughter.

I screamed "No!" as I ran into my room and slammed the door. I let the slam of the door drown out her words as I reached for my pillow. It took a few minutes for the tears to start. They had been stuck in the echoes of that slamming door, or perhaps before that, in the shadows I had sensed around my house. When they finally started, I didn't know if and when they would ever stop.

It was a horrible day. And when I think back on it, one of my clearest memories was of how I had sensed it. I liked to think it was my grandmother I intuited, trying to soften the blow of the news before I had even encountered it.

So why didn't I sense the accident that day? Where was my heightened intuition? Gersonides would say I wasn't receiving the overflow of the Active Intellect. In modern terms, I was disconnected from God. But why?

Slowly, things started to come back to me. I remembered how desperate I had been prior to the accident. I remembered that I had felt like I was lost in a strange town, frantically searching every tunnel and alley for a way back. No matter how hard I searched, I couldn't find philosophic proof for the existence of God – much less a personal God.

So that's what had disconnected me from God; my search for a rational proof. There was something in that search that tore all ties to my former faith. And I remembered the intensity of the search. It had taken over my life. Of course I couldn't sense that something would go wrong that day; I probably couldn't even tell if I was wearing matching socks. When I slammed the door on God, I locked myself into a small confined area where nothing but reason was allowed in. I was obsessed to the point of oblivion with the contents of my own mind, and not much beyond it.

But then I reflected on my state of mind after the accident. I had found something, but I wasn't quite sure what. Maybe it was a small fracture in my skull that allowed my mind to let itself *out*. I still couldn't prove the existence of God, but I could feel it. I felt it in my scarred knee. I felt it in my weak memory that had been wiped clean by a concussion. But mostly, I felt it deep within my gut, where you feel the love for a child. What was that feeling? Where did it emerge from? It wasn't an intellectual decision. It wasn't based on rational arguments. It was an intuition: The same intuition that had warned me about my grandmother's death so many years before.

CHAPTER TWELVE

Long Division

MY JOURNEY HAD taken an unexpected turn. I had started with the intention of figuring out the meaning behind suffering in general, and my accident in particular, but I ended up taking a detour. I was still curious about suffering, but with this new-found interest in intuition, I was eager to explore its meaning in more depth.

I wanted to know what it really was, how it compared to intellectual knowledge, and what role, if any, God played in it. But I was on unfamiliar turf. The medieval rationalists tended to be intellect junkies. Anything below the level of the intellect was coming second in the race to God – and a far second. Intellectual knowledge was the path to understanding God, and intuition (as I had come to understand it) did not come into play. I needed to explore the caverns of modern philosophical thought to locate this elusive concept.

Descartes was known as the father of modern philosophy because he was partly responsible for liberating the world of its Aristotelian stronghold. I always admired Descartes for his daring and his ability to think completely outside of the box. With a quick stroke of his pen he set Greek philosophy to its knees, opening the door for new directions in philosophy. And the cool thing about Descartes was that he did it with flair.

Descartes invited his readers to go through his meditations with him. He started by asserting that as a youth, he adopted false opinions and built his knowledge on the basis of these opinions. He concluded that it was necessary to erase all of his previous conceptions and build again from new foundations. But it would take years to go through every misconception. So, Descartes decided to cut them down from their roots. He claimed that most of these conceptions were based on sensory data. Thus, he began by doubting all knowledge he acquired through his senses. This was no small thing. He set out to prove that you cannot rely on your eyes or ears or any of your senses to obtain true knowledge.

He started by making the observation that, often in his sleep, he dreamed that he was sitting in his chair despite the fact that he was clearly in his bed. He was obviously receiving false information through his dreams. But there were no clear signs that distinguished his sleeping state from his wakeful one. He was astonished to observe that he had no idea whether he was awake or asleep. (Haven't we all had the experience of being asleep and thinking we were awake? They are, admittedly, creepy experiences.) Well, who's to say then that our hands and eyes and feet are real? Perhaps they are part of a dream.

Descartes doubted the absolute reality of just about everything, with the exception of his own mind. He could not doubt the existence of his own mind because he could not deny the obvious fact that he was thinking about these doubts at this very moment! The fact that he was thinking proved that he existed, thus his most famous quotation, "*Cogito ergo sum*," or "I think therefore I am."

Prior to coming to his astonishing conclusions in his *Meditations*, in his first published work, *Discourse on Method*, Descartes lays out rules by which one constructs a philosophical system. Descartes proposes that one should reduce complicated propositions to their simplest components – the intuitive ones. These are the propositions that are self evident, for example, when your nine-year-old comes to you with a problem in long division, you might first tell her not to panic. Long division can be broken up into smaller problems of short division. And short division is just the reverse of multiplication, which is really just addition, but longer. So if you can do addition, you can do long division. Your child might roll her eyes, figure out that you simply forgot how to do long division, and go to her father (which might be a good idea), but what you have done is reduced the long division to its simplest intuitive parts.

According to Descartes, $1+1=2$ is an intuitive proposition. It is known by the "light of reason" and is agreed upon by all humanity. It does not require complicated philosophical proof to demonstrate.

Descartes was my first step toward understanding the concept of intuition. Intuition is the knowledge of self-evident principles – not the hokey emotional "gut feelings" we usually associate with the word. What I had unconsciously discovered after the accident – that inexplicable flash of insight – was something that lies outside of the realm of philosophy departments in universities. It was something that all of mankind has simply perceived.

After Descartes, rationalist philosophers developed their own unique philosophical systems, as opposed to working within the Aristotelian framework. Perhaps this bold break was what inspired Baruch Spinoza, born to a traditional Jewish family in Amsterdam in the seventeenth century, to part with his kinfolks' traditions. He was eventually ex-communicated by the Jews of Holland, and for good reason. Some scholars have labeled him the father of modern atheism.

Spinoza believed that the entire structure of the universe, taken as a whole, is God; in other words, God is Nature. He isn't the miracle-working deity of the Bible. He isn't even the ingenious creator in the sense of *The Book of Genesis*. God is the basic substance of the universe; in fact He is the only substance. Individual things within the universe are just a part or a mode of God, similar to a cog on an intricate machine. God has infinite modes, and you and I are simply two of these modes within God, as is Spinoza.

Spinoza's overall scheme is a deterministic one. Man, as a mode in this elaborate program called God/Nature, has no real control over his actions or desires, just as the cog on the machine has no control over its movement. The laws of the universe follow the necessity of the nature of God. Just as a triangle, by its nature, has three sides, the universe by its nature functions according to certain rules. There is no way to change the workings of the universe (or God). Man is controlled by these laws, which means that all of his actions are predetermined.

It is a bleak view, at least for us Western, Judeo-Christian control freaks, of the role of man in the universe. But Spinoza allows man some form of personal redemption; a person can't break the determinism she falls under, but she *can* become enlightened by understanding it. It seems like a small comfort for someone who has just found out that everything she has achieved in life is not due to her hard work, or elevated intelligence, but is instead part of a scheme that is not at all under her control, or influenced by her deeds, moral, good, or otherwise.

According to Spinoza, good and evil don't truly exist, because everything is part of this perfect scheme called Nature/God. Good and evil are relative notions brought about by man's assessment. If I believe that getting hit by a car is evil, I label it "evil." That in no way implies that it is truly evil. It is simply part of the scheme of nature. But when suffering is understood in light of its role in the scheme of nature, man becomes enlightened – and the evil dissipates, since it never really was.

In Judaism, when one hears about a tragedy, he is supposed to utter the phrase, "*Baruch Dayan haEmet*" which means, "Blessed is the True Judge." It can be a difficult thing to say at times. I remember hearing about the shocking death of a teacher. She was a very unique person. When she had started to teach in my high school, the principal gave her the most difficult kids, because she was the kind of woman who could really make a difference in their lives. She embodied warmth and acceptance. She was the kind of teacher you only get once in your lifetime. She had recently gotten married. The tragic irony of a woman just about to embark on a life with her soul-mate and then dying of a sudden rare disease hit me very hard. I tried to say the words "*Baruch Dayan haEmet*," but my throat was not cooperating. When I finally managed to get it out, I had to say it over and over and over again to myself until I could finally believe it.

Many claim that "*Baruch Dayan haEmet*" is a statement acknowledging that everything that happens is for the good. But that isn't what it literally means. "Blessed is the True Judge" does not make a claim about the goodness of a situation. It just makes a claim about the truthfulness or the justice of a situation. It is really simply the assertion that everything is as it should be, because God is running the show. "Good" and "evil," at least in the 'tragic loss' sense (as opposed to the moral one), are terms that belong to us. They don't belong to the realm of Ultimate Truth.

There was another aspect to Spinoza's thought that interested me: his concept of intuition. According to Spinoza, intuition is the most sublime form of knowledge. (Sense perception and reason are the other two forms.) Intuitive knowledge is the understanding of the unity of Nature's scheme. By understanding the essences of things, their true causes, and their places within the universe, one achieves intuition. This is the supreme perspective of God. When man achieves this type of understanding, man has achieved complete happiness, and intellectual love of God. For Spinoza, intuition is enlightenment.

This was a concept that I could really relate to. Intuition as the road to understanding and loving God was exactly the model I had been seeking. But for Spinoza, this was an intellectual form of intuition. I didn't quite understand how something intellectual could lead to a supreme form of love. Love is an emotion, not the result of philosophic contemplation. Spinoza lived a very cerebral life. He lived largely on the outskirts of society and made a meager living out of crafting lenses (which he apparently excelled at.) He never married, nor did he have children. He had good friends and even some followers. But it struck me that he probably never experienced a burning passion. He described a love of God, but I suspect he truly meant a complete comprehension, like when a scientist suddenly finds that all of his experiments have fallen into place.

Was this the intuition I had found after my accident? It didn't really fit. I didn't suddenly understand things that I had never understood. If anything, I understood fewer things than I ever had. I had *felt* something after my accident that I had never felt before. It was an experience I sought, not an intellectual understanding. I needed to dig further.

CHAPTER THIRTEEN

A Little Duckling in a Row of Ducks

THIS LAST ANALYSIS of intuition brought me to Henri Bergson. Bergson was born in 1859 to Jewish parents, and his faithfulness to his people was to be tested at the end of his life. He became a successful and popular philosopher, so much so that when he visited New York for the first time, he was responsible for Broadway's first traffic jam. When World War One broke out, he was sent by the French government to help President Wilson form the League of Nations. Thus, the philosopher became a politician.

But it was the end of his life that forced him to take his toughest stand. When World War II broke out, the Vichy government offered him an exemption from the anti-Semitic laws. He refused, gave up his honors and titles, and registered himself as a Jew. The story becomes more incredible when one considers that at the time he was rumored to have adopted the Roman Catholic religion.

But it wasn't Bergson's impressive life that first drew me to him. It was his notion of intuition.

Bergson described two types of knowledge – scientific and intuitive. Scientific knowledge derives from analysis. A physicist stands outside an object and seeks to understand it by attributing principles to explain its behavior, giving it measurements, and comparing it to things that he already understands. His knowledge of that object might change if his position changes. So, he might make certain measurements from one angle and then have to make new measurements from another. In this way, his knowledge is relative – it changes depending on his circumstances.

But the second type of knowledge (intuitive knowledge) is not relative. It doesn't change based on the physicist's position, because the physicist is no longer standing outside the object and observing it. With intuitive knowledge, the physicist stands *inside* the object, and gets a completely objective understanding of it. Now he does not need to apply any scientific concepts like measurement to gain an understanding of the object, for he *is* the object.

Bergson gives an example. Consider, he says, a character in a novel. The author describes the character as being six feet tall, balding, and wearing thick glasses. But we don't truly experience him until we start to feel like we are inside of him. Then we can capture him all at once as opposed to enumerating each of his individual characteristics. And only then can we truly understand him, predict how he will behave, and experience emotions with him. Once we become the character, we can truly understand him.

I think Bergson was on to something. I have often had the experience of reading a great novel and coming out feeling completely exhausted. I somehow feel that I've gone through all of the experiences the character went through. It is those books that stay with me the most. That is intuitive knowledge. Intuitive knowledge has no use for symbols and measurements and descriptions. It is not relative knowledge like science. Intuitive knowledge is knowledge of things as they are, not as they appear to the human intellect.

Intuition, then, is absolute knowledge. The most obvious type of intuitive knowledge is knowledge of the self. According to Bergson, this type of knowledge is the subject of metaphysics.

But knowledge of the self isn't the only subject of intuition. Take the concept of time, for example. We tend to understand time by dividing it into small components like seconds, minutes, and hours. In other words, we understand time by standing outside of it (so to speak) and scientifically quantifying it.

But according to Bergson, that is not real time. Real time is a continuous flow, an ever-rolling stream, a duration. Think of time as a perpetually flowing river rather than an Olympic pool that is divided into ten lanes. Time in itself is not divided into lanes; those are things that the Olympic committee imposed. We can only truly understand the nature of time by becoming directly conscious of it rather than intellectually analyzing it. We can understand time by integrating our past, present, and future into one whole experience. The best example is that of a tune. We don't hear the notes of a tune independently and distinctly of one another, we hear them as one unified song, where one note melts into the other. A tune is not a collection of separate entities; it is one duration. Time is similar. It is not a collection of separate events; it is one unified duration. And knowledge of this type of time is called intuition.

I think a good everyday way of understanding Bergson's concept of time is what we call memories. Think of yourself looking through a favorite photo album. You flip through the pages and you spot the picture of your two-year-old in a T-shirt stained with chocolate milk, and a Huggies diaper. She's riding her wooden rocking horse (the one your dad made for her when she was born) with a huge cowboy hat covering her face. You smile in just the way you smiled when you snapped the picture and for a moment you could hear her giggling and smell her baby shampoo.

Or you see that picture of yourself with your best friends at that Italian restaurant that closed years ago. But when you are looking at the picture, the restaurant is no longer closed. You can taste the spaghetti with the garlic cream sauce, and the vanilla ice cream shake. You can hear your friends laughing at the waiter (it was clearly his first day on the job) and you laugh along. The past is no longer an event that happened at one point in your life. It is a living, breathing event that you are experiencing now. The past has melted into the present and effectively destroyed all artificial boundaries. Time is no longer composed of a distinct past and present. Time has been redefined.

Philosophically speaking, Bergson is best understood as a response to Kant. Kant believed that we can only know things that are in time and space. Metaphysics (questions like, Does God exist?) stands proudly outside those two realms, according to Kant, so it is off-limits to human understanding. This was my original problem with Kant prior to my accident; I'd felt that he was closing too many doors and opening too many others.

Bergson claims that Kant is incorrect on both fronts. First, Kant's definition of time only accounts for the artificial scientific understanding of time. Kant is talking about the time on my watch with the black leather strap. For

Bergson, this is not true time. True time is the time we experience, not the time we measure.

Kant's second error, according to Bergson, concerned the inaccessibility of metaphysics. While Bergson agreed with Kant that the intellect cannot penetrate the secrets of metaphysics (and therefore prove the existence of God), he believed that there is a human faculty that can: intuition. Intuition is the ability to understand things in a non-intellectual fashion. Intuition is what grasps the non-rational. It is the difference between a technical writer and a poet. It is the difference between an art teacher and an artist. It is the difference between a scholar and a philosopher. And in my case, it was the difference between an atheist and a believer. With the reintroduction of metaphysics into the realm of the human understanding, the existence of God became something knowable, or should I say: intuited.

But for me, intuition was not only the key to discovering God, it was also the key to understanding myself – as Bergson explained. I was never really in touch with this non-rational (or should I say: supra-rational) element of my being. I have always been supremely intellectual. And to be perfectly honest, I never valued any other type of thought.

It had never occurred to me that maybe this emotional side is another form of intelligence. (The whole "emotional intelligence quotient" idea came to light years later.) It had never occurred to me that emotion might actually be a key component to understanding the universe's deepest mysteries.

Rudolf Otto was a nineteenth-century German theologian who set out to identify the common experience of all religions. He wasn't interested in what distinguished one religion from another; he was more interested in what was similar among the religions. He analyzed the *feeling* of the general religious experience.

He begins his book, *The Idea of the Holy,* by analyzing the word "holy." After dismissing the moral quality that the common understanding of the word indicates (most people think it means "goodness"), he concludes that "holy" is *sui generis.* Meaning, it is completely unique. He cannot find any phrases that adequately embody the entire context of the word. So he invents a word that he would use to understand the concept of "holy," and that word is "numinous." The numinous, he explains, cannot be taught – it must be evoked. He begs the reader to evoke a moment of deep religious experience, and to try to analyze it with him.

The analysis is fascinating, but the critical part for me was the notion that religion cannot be confined to everyday vocabulary. I would have to draw on something outside of my words, outside of my rational thought, in order to properly grasp its meaning. Religion is primarily a non-rational (as opposed to irrational) experience, and it needs to be understood that way.

When I read Otto, it struck me that I had been so busy trying to find a rational philosophical proof for the existence of God that I never stopped to ask myself some basic questions: Isn't my knowledge of God somehow different from rational knowledge? Isn't it different from my cold cognition of the square root of a number? Isn't it somehow warmer? Isn't it more personal? Isn't it more integral to my being? Doesn't it touch the very core my soul? And if it doesn't, if it isn't, why am I so disturbed by not being able to find it?

They were stunning admissions. They pointed to a person who had previously been completely oblivious to her own nature, and the true meaning of faith. And now that I could finally ask the questions, I needed to understand the answers.

But how does one go about opening up a channel of her mind that had never been broadcast on before? How could I begin to experience things in a way that couldn't be summed up by philosophical argument? Otto suggested evoking a deeply religious moment. After hours of head banging and hair pulling, I finally came up with something: Yom Kippur.

I was in that wonderful teenage stage of oblivion; I was old enough to appreciate the importance of the day, but I didn't let it intimidate me. Yom Kippur arrived, and I slipped off my comfortable leather shoes, and put on my less comfortable canvas ones. I finished the big meal prior to the start of the holiday, brushed my teeth, and thought to myself with a degree of consternation that this would be the last time I would be able to brush them in twenty-four hours. (On Yom Kippur there are five things that are prohibited to Orthodox Jews: food and drink, leather shoes, bathing, creams and make-up, and sexual intercourse.) I met my mother downstairs and we walked to synagogue.

We would spend the majority of the next twenty-four hours there, praying.

I entered and made my way down the carpeted aisle to the birch wood bench in the third row which I shared every year with my mother, aunt, and cousin. There was nervousness in the air. The tension was palpable. People were concerned about making it through the long fast. But that wasn't all. Jews believe that Yom Kippur is the day that God seals our fates for the year ahead. In theory, we spend the first ten days of the Jewish month of Tishrei in repentance, culminating with Yom Kippur.

The fact is, many don't do the appropriate soul-searching until the day of Yom Kippur and were probably regretting it now.

But it is more than that. Something strange happens every Yom Kippur. The air is laced with the scent of contradiction. Everyone who enters the synagogue smells it. Yom Kippur is a multi-dimensional day. Like most of the Jewish holidays, it reflects antinomy, the dialectic of sadness and joy that washes over most things the Jewish people do.

Passover, for example, is a day of rejoicing. It celebrates Jewish liberation from Egypt. But, we are told, that there is also an element of sadness. We eat bitter herbs (often ground-up white horseradish), and dip potatoes in salt water, to commemorate the slavery and bitterness of the lives of the Jewish people in Egypt.

The Jewish wedding day is similarly conflicted. For the bride and groom it is one of the happiest days of their lives. But it is also a day of introspection. They say the same confessional prayers that we say on Yom Kippur. And under the wedding canopy, the groom breaks a glass in commemoration of the saddest day of the Jewish calendar, the day the Temple was destroyed. This is a physical act that represents the couple's commitment to the national destiny of the Jewish people.

On Yom Kippur, too, our emotions are woven with contradictory threads. It is a day devoted to honest self-reflection, which in itself is a paradoxical process. Stripping yourself down to your basic characteristics, identifying your core motives, seeing yourself raw and exposed, can be confusing and even disturbing. There will be things you are proud of and things you are most definitely not proud of. There are strengths you never knew you had, but there are also limitations you have never come to terms with. On Yom Kippur, you begin to accept yourself, but in the same breath you vow to work on yourself.

On Yom Kippur God is both comforting and frightening. On the one hand, He is at your side – present in the low hum of the congregation, and the swaying of the prayer shawls. He is in the quiet sobs of the repentant, and the poetry of the prayers. But on the other hand, God is the objective Decider of your fate. He knows all and forgets nothing. He could not be more distant or more terrifying.

Yom Kippur is a day of elation, and it is a day of profound regret. It is a day of revelation; and it is a day of deep mystery. Like a complicated work of literature, Yom Kippur is intimidating, yet inviting. We don't want it to start, but we don't want it to end. It is a day that defies intellectual categories. Yom Kippur must be felt, not understood.

That particular Yom Kippur of my teenage-hood, I reached my row, placed my prayer book on the shelf in front of me, and looked ahead to the front of the synagogue. I was looking for someone in particular in the front row. She had arrived before me. She stood frail and vulnerable, like a kitten in a forest of lions, close to the wall that separated the men from the women. She was an older woman who had lived through the Holocaust and the birth of the State of Israel. I looked for her whenever I went to synagogue because we had a special relationship. It wasn't acknowledged in words. It was a smile, or knowing look, or the shake of the hand. I couldn't explain why, but somehow I felt that she could see into my soul. I sat down once I saw her, amazed at her stamina. She was so old and brittle, and yet she was always there.

The day went as every other Yom Kippur did. It started a little stiffly, like when you first open a book, before you get into the characters. But the first long silent prayer began to open me up. A silent prayer (one that is said quietly to yourself) is more effective to begin with, at least for me. It gives you a sense that you are whispering in God's ear, as opposed to standing in the middle of a crowded synagogue. Secrets need to be whispered, at least at first. By the end of the day, you will be shouting them as loud as you can in an attempt to convince God (and yourself) that you mean to change. But at the beginning, it just comes in whispers. Each prayer exposes new things about yourself, with building intensity.

By the end of day, the fasting minions grow weary. Weary of standing in synagogue after a long, emotionally harsh day. Weary of the hunger and thirst plaguing them throughout the twenty-four hours. Weary of their neighbors, who either make too much noise or too little. But the last hour of the day is like a horse race. Every year, the congregants try to get in their last prayers while God remains beside them.

That Yom Kippur, we could sense His slow ascent, and it terrified us. Had we done enough? Had we said what needed to be said? The prayers ended with a confident note, but rare was the congregant who could really *feel* confident. The piercing shofar blast marked God's final ascent. We felt bereft of His company, but eager to return home.

That particular year, however, I found my eyes searching that front row again. Was she still there? Had she held out until the end? There she stood, the littlest duckling in a row of ducks, her eyes glowing like two black jewels reflecting the sun. Our eyes met briefly and I saw her mouth the words, "Yom Kippur is my favorite day." I let myself absorb her remark before I mouthed back, "Mine, too." Then I smiled to myself, because I knew that I had meant it.

Yom Kippur is not a day to be analyzed scientifically. It is a day beyond rational thought. It is a day to be intuited. We sense God's presence in the ethereal air that surrounds us. Scientists might find a link between religious observance and a sense of spirituality. Perhaps they could measure it, quantify it, or rank it. But science can't tell me anything about Yom Kippur. I needed to experience it myself.

Otto was right. Religion is best defined by an experience, not a philosophical proof. I know there is a God because I experience Him. And now I finally had my much sought-after definition of intuition: intuition is the first moment you smell jasmine, just before you try to describe it. Intuition is that breathless instant of love at first sight, the briefest seconds where you still don't know what hit you. Intuition is what grasps our experiences before our intellect can sink its teeth into them. Intuition was my key to understanding faith.

When I think back on this Yom Kippur experience, I remember the religious problems that I had encountered prior to the accident. Kant had disproved the arguments for the existence of God. I remember how distraught I had become to learn of Kant's criticisms of them. I remember how disillusioned I had been at this surgical separation of faith from reason. But I had missed the point entirely.

It suddenly occurred to me that Kant's *real* point when he claimed to have saved faith by getting rid of reason was simply this: Faith and reason can't occupy the same chair. And despite the fact that Kant's view of God ultimately differed drastically from a religious perspective (he believed in God as a postulate of ethics), he did religion a huge favor by cutting it free from the fist of reason. It's not that he couldn't prove the existence of God, it's that he couldn't prove it the same way he went about proving everything else.

God's realm is not in reason. It is in something deeper and more profound. It is in something that I had to work a lot harder at. But I intuited Him that day on my birch wood bench.

PART THREE

CHAPTER FOURTEEN

Elihu's Tale, Continued

Elihu was eager to continue his tale but he forced himself to stop and contemplate it further. He knew that the most critical section still needed to be written, and he had to think hard about how he wanted to convey his message. His rational side decided that it was best to wait until the next day to continue with his story. But the thin wooden table in the corner, with the parchments strewn about, kept calling to him. The creative side of his brain longed to get the story told. It was tugging at him like a child pulling on his mother's shirt. He didn't want to risk losing his muse, so he eventually gave in.

That night was a perfectly clear one. The sky resembled a dark cave with tiny candles perched in the crevices. But the moon was the true master of the night. Its light burned fiercer than the flames of the Temple. Elihu had never seen a moon like this before. The contrast between the black night and the intense glow of the moon was so distinct, it seemed almost deliberate. It was as if the moon was trying to stand up and make a statement. Elihu took in the crisp night air and then returned to his tent to pick up where he had left off...

The wind raged in every direction, almost knocking Job over. At first he could see nothing. He was a blind man in a cyclone. But slowly he made out a faint glimmer of light. He understood at once that he was looking at the moon. The moon looked remarkably dim that night: as if its light had been blown out by that powerful storm. He felt strangely connected to the moon; it perfectly reflected the state of his soul. Job stood, holding onto the tent, and was almost knocked over by the sheer force of the wind. It was like nothing he had ever experienced before. And then he heard a voice. It came at him like a clap of thunder. The voice of God was unbearable.

"Who is this beseeching me? Where was he when I established the foundations of the universe?"

God's question silenced Job. More than the message, the force of the voice simply terrified him. It took a few minutes for the meaning of God's words to become clear.

Job swallowed hard as if to quell the pounding of his heart by the action. He was overcome by the intensity of his own insignificance. He realized for the first time how limited he really was . . .

But none of it mattered.

He just wanted it to end. He put his hands over his ears to block out the voice. But then the voice did something puzzling. It challenged Job with a riddle: "There is a kind of bird that abandons her eggs in the dust. She abandons them and disowns them. In her eyes they are not her babies. And yet, they survive."

Was it a metaphor? But Job knew that there was indeed such a bird. He had often wondered how that species of bird could survive. Who feeds these baby birds and who protects them? Who teaches them to fly and hunt? In fact he himself had tried once to save some of them. He thought he would give them to his children as pets. But eventually they flew away. It was as if they had their own mechanisms of survival built in. But that was his answer, wasn't it? If they were born with these mechanisms, then God put them there. He was their creator. God knew their nature and supplied them with the means to continue. God didn't abandon them like their mothers had. He taught them how to cope.

Was that the solution to God's message? Was he somehow trying to teach Job to cope? But how? He hadn't given Job the physical means to cope with his losses the way He had with the birds. All He gave Job was this meeting . . .

Job was silent. He was waiting for permission to speak, and God encouraged him to do so.

"Ask, Job, and I will answer," He promised. But then He Himself continued.

"Are you going to call Me wicked to prove your righteousness? The two are not mutually exclusive, Job. I never denied your righteousness."

Job felt slightly vindicated. His sufferings couldn't be an indictment of his actions, because God admitted that he had done nothing wrong. But then he grew more confused. Then WHY???

God continued to talk about His awesome creations and Job stood and listened. What else could he do? Almost without realizing it, he was beginning to perceive God differently. God was no longer a remote being who afflicted man at will. God's voice was becoming softer and softer. Was that Him lowering His voice, or Job getting used to it? Job wondered. Job uncovered his ears to listen. Slowly he was coming to the realization that God just wanted to talk with him.

And then a strange thing happened. Job started to feel a little bit better. He began to understand what his soul really longed for. He realized that he was not searching for information; he was searching for consolation. He didn't need to know why; he needed to know that there was a "why." He needed reassurance that God was there, even when his children were gone. And for the first time in days, Job's body stopped shaking.

CHAPTER FIFTEEN

Broken Ladders

WHEN KANT CEASED to haunt me, Elisha Ben Abuya took over. Elisha Ben Abuya was one of the greatest Talmudic minds amid the pantheon of righteous scholars in his day. Unfortunately, he was also, ultimately, one of the most fervent apostates Judaism has ever produced. One account in the Talmud explains his apostasy with the following story:

One day Elisha ben Abbuya was walking with his student Rabbi Meir and they came upon a father and a son. They overheard the father asking the son to retrieve eggs from a nest perched atop of a house. The father set up a ladder, reminded his son to shoo away the mother bird before grabbing the eggs, as prescribed by the Torah, and sent his son on this mission. Elisha Ben Abuya pointed out to his student that surely this boy would live a long life because he was following two commandments from the Torah that promised their adherents long lives – honoring thy father, and sending away the mother bird to spare her the pain of losing her eggs. They continued to look on, as the boy started to climb the ladder. Then they heard a devastating crash. The ladder had broken, and the boy had fallen to his death.

Elisha Ben Abuya's world came crashing down with that ladder. He lost his faith and denounced God's existence. I had never met Elisha ben Abuya, but if I had, I'd bet his eyes were completely colorless, having lost their color with his loss of faith. I had been in his shoes once. I had stopped believing in God and had felt the color drain from my eyes.

Judaism lost a great scholar that day. The fact is the problem of the righteous suffering had been a thorn in man's thigh since the creation of Adam. Moses himself questioned God about justice in this world, and God's response was obscure. It seems that this is a question we are destined to struggle with. Doubtless, Judaism has lost many of its believers to this problem; but did those who searched and remained gain something from their search?

My journey toward finding a solution had turned into a maze with many paths. The first path: rediscovering God outside the confines of my intellect. It was one of the most difficult things I ever had to do. Suddenly I had to stop thinking and start feeling. It was like teaching a computer to cry. (To be honest, I still struggle with it at times.) But it was a crucial piece of the puzzle that was requisite to continuing my journey. It was only with a strong faith in God and a healthy dose of the awareness of the limitations of the human intellect that my search could go on. Immanuel Kant would never know it, but he was my first step toward coming to terms with human suffering.

But as I made strides towards understanding my faith in God, Elisha Ben Abuya's questions loomed larger. How could God, who claimed to be compassionate and good, the same God who sat next to me on that birch wood bench on Yom Kippur, kill a child as he was listening to his father? How could the very commandment that promised to grant long life *take* the life of a child? And why would God allow a taxi cab to hit a perfectly innocent young woman standing on the corner of 34th Street? Kant wasn't the final path to this maze. Neither were the medieval thinkers I had examined previously. Saadya's stance regarding the innate perfection of divine justice, Maimonides's emphasis on the human causes of suffering and advanced intellectual immunity to it, and Gersonides's theory of Divine providence all provided clues, but they couldn't provide adequate overall solutions. These answers were simply colored threads in a larger, more intricate tapestry that I had yet to finish weaving.

CHAPTER SIXTEEN

Reading the Book Backwards

I REMEMBER A CHILDREN'S book that I once read called *Reflections*. The book is unique in that it could be read in two directions – front to back and back to front. It is written in the voice of a child who is reflecting on her day by the sea. When you read it front to back, it is a description of the morning and early afternoon. It describes the dawn with its early rising fishermen and empty boatyards. It continues with the mid-morning packed beaches, and orchard trees with ripe peaches. But as you near the end of the book, the character turns around, indicating to the reader that he too should turn the book around. Now the book is read in the opposite direction. The character describes the late afternoon, dusk, and evening periods at the sea: the carnivals, the frogs in the pond, dinner at the restaurant, and the setting sun.

When I reflected upon it, I realized that the multi-directional character of the book is similar to the way the universe functions. Things in this world can be looked at from two completely different perspectives. This was the realization that finally brought me some closure. It was the philosophy of Rabbi Josef Soloveitchik that first introduced me to this way of thinking about the world.

Rabbi Joseph Ber Soloveitchik was born to an elite family of Torah scholars in 1903 in what was then Russia. Under his father and grandfather's careful tutelage, he adopted an intensely rigorous method of studying Talmud and Jewish law. From his mother, he learned to experience the warmth and beauty of Judaism. She also exposed him to secular literature, and he eventually went to study in Berlin and earned a PhD in philosophy. Rabbi Soloveitchik was one of the few modern Torah scholars who achieved excellence in both Jewish and secular modes of learning. His philosophy was an example of how secular knowledge can help elucidate Torah ideas.

Rabbi Soloveitchik's essay, entitled "The Voice of My Beloved is Knocking" (the title deriving from a verse in the *Song of Songs*) was the essay that altered the course of my investigation, and my life. It was a long, warm bath for my aching mind.

Rabbi Soloveitchik would use prototypes, or "straw men," to elucidate his philosophy of Judaism. His essays would speak of "cognitive man," "homo-religiosus" (religious man), or "halakhic (Jewish law) man." People often make the mistake of trying to find themselves, or someone they know, in Rabbi Soloveitchik's characters, but that is misguided. It is similar to trying to find someone exactly like Charlie Brown. We all have some Charlie Brown in us, but are there any real *actual* Charlie Browns among us? (Besides myself, of course . . .)

Rabbi Soloveitchik's characters are extremes, not real people. They represent the elements that are found within us, but not exclusively. Rabbi Soloveitchik recognizes that people often contain conflicting characteristics. He knows that people are complex. In order to understand them, he isolates certain characteristics and creates prototypes from them. These prototypes are the models through which he teaches his readers about the philosophy behind Jewish law.

In "The Voice of My Beloved is Knocking," Rabbi Soloveitchik creates two prototypes: the 'Man of Fate' and the 'Man of Destiny.' These two different kinds of people correspond to two ways of approaching suffering. The first explains his bad fortune away as fate, and the second embraces it as a way of achieving destiny. The first asks "Why me?"; the second asks, "What now?"

The Man of Fate has resigned himself to what he perceives as his lot in life. He feels himself to be part of a larger scheme that is blind and unpredictable. He encounters suffering in two stages. First he is shocked into silence. He feels that the forces of the universe have conspired against him and he is helpless. He sinks into a depression that completely silences him. But once the initial shock wears off, he sets himself on a course of intellectual investigation. He is bothered by the evil in the world, and he desperately wants to believe that the universe is basically good. He encounters metaphysical theories that explain away or intellectualize evil, much like the medieval philosophers we encountered in earlier chapters. Evil doesn't exist, he concludes, and continues to live a life of self-deception.

In doing so, Rabbi Soloveitchik argues, the fatalist is denying the obvious. There is unexplainable evil in the world! This man himself has experienced it. Call it privation; call it an excuse for a reward in the world to come; call it whatever you please – it is evil. Perhaps from the infinite perspective of God, there is no true evil – but how many of us have the benefit of that perspective? From the human perspective, there is no use denying the evil and suffering that we experience.

The Man of Fate simply fools himself. He makes the fatal mistake of asking a question that has no answer. He asks himself, "Why did this happen to me?" He asks himself, "How can there be evil in the world?" (Sound familiar?) He makes his investigation an inquiry into the metaphysics of evil. And then he tricks himself into accepting his fate. As such, his journey is doomed to failure from the outset.

What he fails to see is that the world is multi-directional, like my children's book. The universe, in a parable quoted by the Rabbi, is like an exquisitely woven rug. But man can only see the rug from the reverse side. He can see all the imperfections, all the snags, and pieces of stray string. But he doesn't have access to the right side. He can't see the beautifully integrated picture. That can only be grasped by someone with an infinite perspective. Man can only read the book backward, not forward. Thus, man's attempt at an inquiry into to the problem of theodicy is inappropriate. The question is simply unanswerable from his perspective.

The Man of Destiny is a very different type of person. He doesn't view himself as a victim of circumstance; he confronts what is dealt to him. The man of Destiny is not an object; he is a subject. He is not passive; he is active. His question in the face of suffering is not "Why?" but "What?" It isn't, "Why does God allow evil to exist?" it is "What can I do with this?" and "What does this mean to me?" He does not deny or question personally experienced evil

– he accepts it and tries to make something out of it. For Rabbi Soloveitchik, this entails repentance.

Rabbi Soloveitchik's answer was ground breaking for me. I had been looking at the problem from the wrong side of the book. I had been searching for philosophical enlightenment. I wanted to know why God did this to me. I wanted to know how evil could exist in a universe created by God. But I was missing the point. I wanted to know the answers to questions that were completely beyond human capacity. I wanted to look directly at the sun without going blind. But I failed to notice that the universe was multi-directional. I couldn't read the book forward, but I could read it backward. I couldn't look at the sun, but I could look at the moon. I couldn't know "why," but I could know "what."

In late 1959, Rabbi Soloveitchik was struck with cancer. This encounter with suffering and his own personal limitations inspired him to write an essay entitled "Out of the Whirlwind." In this essay, he further explicated the dynamics of his theory of suffering.

Ultimately, suffering reinvigorates man, according to Rabbi Soloveitchik. When man suffers, he goes through stages. First, he confronts his own mortality. We all know intellectually that one day we will die. We write wills, buy burial plots, and plan for our eventual demise. But do we really know it? Do we feel it in our bones? Or do we acknowledge it, but internally remain convinced that, somehow, we will live forever?

Man doesn't have a true understanding of what it means to be mortal until he gets sick. Sickness bestows upon man the existential awareness that one day he will die; he begins to feel it in his bones. This is the most frightening awareness that you can experience. When man becomes aware, not just intellectually aware, but emotionally and instinctively aware, of his own mortality, he truly suffers.

Rabbi Soloveitchik relates his own personal trial with a story about his bout with cancer. He describes himself prior to the cancer as thinking of himself as a contemporary to his grandson. Death and human limitation somehow didn't apply to him. Then he describes the night prior to his surgery. He prayed to God just to grant him the ability to attend his daughter's wedding – an event that had been pushed off because of his surgery. He realized how he had been knocked down to size. Before his illness, he was an eternal being; now he'd be happy just to make it to the wedding. But Rabbi Soloveitchik calls this "fall from the heights of an illusory immortality . . . the greatest achievement of the long hours of anxiety and uncertainty." He had acknowledged the message of his sickness. This new awareness of one's limitations is critical in self-development. Only when you are brought down to size, are you ready to face your mission in life.

Rabbi Soloveitchik goes on to explain that everyone was put on this earth at a specific time and place in order to fulfill a certain role. But it is only with the knowledge of your own finitude that you can begin to buckle down and concentrate on the role you were put on this earth to play.

When I read this, I had to stop and look around because I had an eerie feeling that Rabbi Soloveitchik was peering over my shoulder. He had described the effects of my accident perfectly. I vividly remember the moment my faith crisis hit, months before the accident.

It was during a class about Maimonides. It has been said that all of Western philosophy is a footnote to Plato. The same could be said of Maimonides. All medieval Jewish philosophy after him was a footnote to his thought. He was the barometer by which you labeled other philosophers. They were either with him, more extreme, less extreme, or against him, but they all contended with him. That day, the teacher was discussing the Active Intellect, which in Aristotle's system was the tenth of the intellects that emanated from God. The Active Intellect was said to receive the ideas emanated from God and use them to control the affairs of men in our world. The Active Intellect was responsible for prophecy and providence. It seemed to me that God played a more indirect role in the functioning of our universe according the medieval rationalists. I sat in my seat writing furiously when it dawned upon me. It was the most frightful thought that had ever seeped into my head. No, it can't be, I thought to myself. But it might be. I raised my hand and gulped out my question:

"So, was the Active Intellect what *we* think of as . . . God?" As soon as I said it I wanted to take it back. It was anti-religious, anti-Jewish, anti-everything I had ever learned about God. In Judaism there was only one God. It was the pinnacle tenet of our faith – one which Maimonides himself listed as essential to faith. The Jews were the ones who introduced monotheism into the world.

How could there be a God, *and* an Active Intellect? The professor looked at me and with that perfectly objective intellectual tone that so characterized philosophical discussion, he unknowingly said the words I so desperately did not want to hear, "Good question!"

I don't think I heard the answer he subsequently proposed because I had already begun my descent. I knew there was no Active Intellect. That was a concept conceived by Aristotle which had since been deemed irrelevant. But Maimonides didn't know that. He believed in it. How did *he* reconcile his faith with his philosophy? Why didn't it seem to pose a problem for him? If the Active Intellect controlled our world, did God have a role in the affairs of individual men according to Maimonides? The answer Maimonides gives was one that I couldn't appreciate until much later. He explains that God does know individuals, but God's knowledge and man's knowledge are two completely different things. So yes, God knows us ... but we don't understand how or what that means.

It seemed to me at the time that Maimonides had taken away any meaningful way of knowing us (providence) and given it to the Active Intellect. What's more, with no Active Intellect on the philosophical scene in our day, and God still being a completely remote principle, it left me wondering who – if anyone – knows man?

And what did all of this mean for my traditional conception of God? Where was the God who was said to have listened to my prayers? Where was the God who was said to be watching me? Where was the God who was said to be speaking to the prophets in the Bible? I left the room that day a completely different person. I had woken up that morning a staunch believer. I had lived the first twenty years of my life a staunch believer. I walked into that classroom that day a staunch believer. But when I left I was something quite different. I had become a doubter.

The immediate and dramatic effects of these ideas on me might seem strange to the average (dare I say "normal?") person. Most people don't take these things as seriously as I do. People can generally distinguish esoteric philosophy from their everyday lives. I remember a conversation I had with a friend concerning our respective majors in college.

"What are you majoring in?" she asked.

"Philosophy," I responded.

"Oh, I took a philosophy class recently. I really enjoyed it. I even considered majoring in it. But you have to grow up at some point, you know. You have to choose something that you can do something with. You know what I mean?"

I stared at her blankly. She might as well have been speaking in some African tribal language with clicks and whistles, because I had no idea what she was meant.

What could be more important in life than questions concerning ultimate reality? The fact was, I had always spent far too much time exploring the expanse vistas of my frighteningly overactive mind. When Descartes questioned the existence of the physical world, the physical world ceased to exist in my mind. And when Kant challenged the proofs for the existence of God . . . well . . . my mind began to play with possibility of a world without God. The crazy thing is, I could live in a world devoid of physical reality (with the possible exception of Carvel ice-cream). But for me, a world without God was a world without meaning. It would be inconceivable to live in a world without meaning.

I've read accounts of former believers becoming doubters. I've read of people slipping in and out of religious belief like it was a sweatshirt. If it felt comfortable one day, they would wear it. If it was too hot the next day, they'd slip it off. It was seamless for them. That wasn't how it was for me. My descent into religious skepticism was fraught with pain and longing. There were days that I rejected God as a religious tactic constructed for the masses; and then there were days when the loneliness was so overwhelming I found myself begging the very God I didn't believe in for enlightenment. Religion wasn't a sweatshirt for me; it was my skin. Slipping in and out of it was excruciating.

Months later, Rabbi Soloveitchik allowed me to see what I hadn't appreciated that day in Maimonides class (and the reason I couldn't really grasp Maimonides' conception of Divine knowledge): my doubts were based on more than just a particular idea – they were based on a flawed, inflated perception of the human intellect. Before Greek philosophy entered the world, people used mythology to explain all the "big questions," such as the origin of the universe. The first Greek philosophers, called pre-Socratics, brought a different mode of thinking to these problems. For the first time, problems were thought out rationally and argued amongst philosophers. It was the birth of rationalism and it claimed that the "big questions" were subjects that our minds can grasp. It was this faith in the role of the intellect that appealed to many medieval Jewish philosophers.

But what some of these medieval religious philosophers didn't appreciate was that strict rationalism was ultimately contrary to religion. Rationalism claimed that all things were subject to intellectual comprehension; religion argued that some things were beyond human comprehension. And while rationalism and religion may complement each other, they do not necessarily arrive at the same truths. Ultimately, rationalism poses challenges to some fundamental religious beliefs, and vice versa. Something has to give in each to allow the other to co-exist. And in Maimonides class that day, my religious convictions started to give.

But why was I so drawn to rationalism as a young adult? There were other strains of philosophical thought that I could have studied. For some reason, these other schools of thought didn't attract me the way rationalism did. There was something about the beauty of the organization of a philosophical argument. There was something about the symmetry and accessibility of it. I loved how one thing logically flowed from another. I loved trying to find the weakness in an argument. I loved the intellectual challenge. But there was more to it than that. I liked the secure feeling that knowledge gave me. It was a sense of control that I craved. It was a way to make sense of the seemingly nonsensical universe. Rationalism was a way of claiming the universe under my wing. It was a way of achieving intellectual immortality.

The car accident really shook me up. It wasn't just the injury to my knee that affected me so badly; it was the injury to my head. It was terrifying. I spent weeks unable to read and concentrate. I couldn't remember things that had happened right before the accident. And once I regained my memory, things only slightly improved.

I was still faced with the fact of the accident to explain. I was forced to encounter something that was completely inexplicable. It was as if God was bringing me down to size. It was as if God was trying to force me to concede defeat. I had encountered my own intellectual finitude, that day on the corner of 34th and Park, and it was terrifying. Rabbi Soloveitchik was indeed peering over my shoulder as I read his section about the role of suffering in shrinking humanity back to appropriate proportions. He knew exactly what I had been thinking.

But according to Rabbi Soloveitchik suffering doesn't only serve to point out an individual's limitations, it also has another profoundly disturbing effect. It secludes man from those around him. Suffering engenders a deep existential loneliness within a person. Rabbi Soloveitchik tells a story about delivering a eulogy for his uncle before an auditorium full of healthy people, while he himself was very ill. He felt singularly distinct from the the members of the audience, a dying rose in a vase of fresh flowers. Suffering isolates man from others. A person who was once a member of a community, a family, a group of friends, begins to perceive herself as lone figure struggling with her own fate. Man stands with his suffering alone, to meet God.

I remember that feeling of isolation. I think I expected the fabric of the universe to be dramatically altered after I emerged from the hospital. I expected people to act differently and to care about different things. I felt that in some way I couldn't have been the only one to have been affected by this. I longed to talk to someone who could understand. But there was nobody. I was astounded to find people going about their everyday lives, even though mine had been so completely altered. Before the accident, my friends and family had been very much a part of me. I couldn't imagine myself detached from them. After the accident, I felt secluded, a bird without her flock. Perhaps that was why I needed to make sense of God's role in this accident. Maybe I needed to reconnect with God because I so desperately needed to talk to *someone* who might understand.

In an essay entitled "Majesty and Humility," Rabbi Soloveitchik relates the following:

> Eleven years ago my wife lay on her deathbed and I watched her dying, day by day, hour by hour. Medically I could do very little for her. All I could do was pray. . . . The moment I returned home I would rush to my room, fall on my knees, and pray fervently. God, in those moments, appeared not as the exalted, majestic king, but rather as a

humble, close friend, brother, father. In such moments of black de-spair, He was not far from me; He was right there in the dark room. I felt His warm hand . . . on my shoulder; I hugged His knees . . . . He was with me in the narrow confines of a small room, taking up no space at all. . . .

CHAPTER SEVENTEEN

Suffering Without Sin

BUT THERE IS another stage to this confrontation with God. Suffering doesn't just break man down; it ultimately raises him up. Once a person becomes aware of her own limitations, she can begin to step out of herself and become aware of realities she's never experienced before. Unable to explain her suffering intellectually, she no longer ties herself to her own intellect, and she begins to explore new vistas of her personality. Ultimately, a confrontation with God elevates a person's spirit.

Victor Frankl writes, "If there is meaning in life at all, then there must be a meaning in suffering" (*Man's Search for Meaning*). According to Frankl, the *way in which man accepts* his suffering enables him to add depth to his life. In the concentration camps during the Holocaust, Frankl witnessed and experienced first-hand the depths that suffering can reach. As a survivor, he asks an interesting, deeply reflective question: What differentiated those who survived from the ones that didn't? It wasn't their physical condition, he noted. Because, he explains, many of the strongest inmates died, while physically weaker ones remained alive. So what was their secret? What allowed the survivors to *survive*?

According to Frankl, the survivors were those who could see past their suffering and could formulate the sentence, "I need to survive because of X." X might be a person, a job, or a calling. X was the reason to endure that allowed these people to live. These were the people with deep inner lives. These were also the people who were able to accept their fates as beyond their control, but to make the personal decision not to forfeit their humanity – something within their control. In Rabbi Soloveitchik's terms, these were people of destiny.

So it was clear to me that I needed to find an X. I needed to figure out what I had to do to allow my suffering to guide and deepen my life. *How could my injury and its aftermath contribute to my humanity?* Rabbi Soloveitchik speaks of repentance and prayer as avenues to mining suffering for meaning. But to me this implied that I had done something wrong. I briefly considered my period as a religious skeptic as the suspect, but I immediately rejected it. That was an error, a stage of intellectual and spiritual growth – not a sin. Did I need to repent for making a philosophical detour on the way to finding God? That didn't sit well with me.

There is a fascinating debate recorded in the Talmud (Tractate Shabbat 55a-b) on this type of question. Rabbi Ammi makes the claim that there is no death or suffering without sin. The Talmud goes on to object that there were four people who died *only* because of the general decree of death bestowed on mankind after the sin of Adam and Eve, and not for anything they had done. These "sinless" individuals were, according to the Talmud, Benjamin the son of Jacob, Amram the father of Moses, Jesse the father of King David, and Kilav the son of King David. In light of these four individuals, the Talmud concludes that there is indeed such a thing as death and suffering without sin.

This section of the Talmud elicited numerous observations. A professor of mine, Rabbi Shalom Carmy, once pointed out that the four sinless individuals listed were actually not big players in the Bible; they were only related to the big players in some way. Thus, it was Jesse who was said to have never sinned, not his son King David; Amram, not his son Moses. The greatest people in the Bible had sinned at some point in their lives. Perhaps this implies that leadership and nobility requires a history of sin, or, perhaps even that it is the sin itself that raises one above the level of a completely pure soul. There is a well-known concept in Jewish tradition that someone who has sinned and repented is greater than someone who has never sinned at all. Is there, in fact, a redemptive quality to sin?

But it was the debate's conclusion that actually fascinated me most: people die and suffer despite the fact that they are without sin. Suffering is clearly not just a mechanism for punishment. What other dimensions lie betwixt its dark and painful creases? Why else would God inflict man with suffering? It is a question that Rabbi Soloveitchik claims has no answer. He says we ought to use suffering as a reminder to simply repent and return to God as dictated by Jewish Law. But what if there is nothing to repent for? It's like taking medication for a disease you don't have. Besides, how would one go about repenting for a sin he couldn't identify? Perhaps redefining what Rabbi Soloveitchik means by repentance is the key.

Rabbi Shalom Carmy addresses this issue in the introduction to a book he edited, entitled *Jewish Perspectives on the Experience of Suffering*. He explains in this work that the question posed is based on a misunderstanding. When you view suffering and sin via a cause-and-effect modality, you are misinterpreting your relationship with God. You don't necessarily suffer because of a specific sin. A relationship with God is more complex than that.

Carmy posits that a relationship with God is similar to a relationship with a close friend. If that friendship goes sour, there isn't always an obvious reason for it. And if you wish to renew the friendship it might not necessarily be about saying you're sorry for a specific action. Instead, you might need to re-evaluate the relationship, express sorrow over its present state, analyze the underlying difficulties, and perhaps even reflect on yourself first. Relationships tend not to be black and white, cause and effect. To suggest that they are devalues them.

Similarly, a relationship with God is ambiguous in nature. To repair it requires self-analysis, and a deeper understanding of God. The effort to renew your relationship will be difficult, even confounding at times, but in the end it will yield a more profound connection.

This new perspective on punishment, as a reflection of the 'state of the union' between ourselves and God, was illuminating for me. Repentance, then, did not necessitate a sin; it could simply mean returning to God humble, and ready to reconnect with a clean, open soul. Perhaps this is what Rabbi Soloveitchik was getting at; suffering removes our pretenses and our defenses and our arrogant assumptions of control. Suffering readies us to pursue our relationship with the Divine from a place of deference, from a place of greater respect for the universe and the fact that it is unknowable.

◆ ◆ ◆

This version of repentance, which sat much better with me, reminded me of a well-known section of the Talmud dealing with suffering. In Tractate Berachot 5a, Rava is recorded as saying that if a man sees that he is suffering, he must first examine his deeds. Deeds represent the moral aspects of life. The implication of the Talmud is that if one's moral values are not up to speed, he will suffer – either as a natural consequence of his immoral life, or as a punishment from God (or perhaps, both. They are not mutually exclusive). But if one should find that his moral values are above reproach, he should examine the amount of time he spends studying the Torah. The study of Torah represents the intellectual aspects of religion. The Talmud posits that when people go astray intellectually, they too will suffer.

I had experienced that type of suffering first hand. My rational mind led me to doubt Judaism's claims, and for a year I felt like I had forfeited my soul to my brain. I was a traitor to my own spirit. Intellectual suffering is as powerful as any car accident. And it is a natural consequence of overvaluing your brain.

But, according to the Talmud, if one can safely say that his morals are proper, and that he maintains a proper perspective concerning his intellect, then he must conclude that his sufferings are "afflictions of love." "Afflictions of love" sounded to me at first like the title of a bad seventies' album, but I was pretty confident that the rabbis of the Talmud were not fans of seventies' pop music. So what were "afflictions of love?"

Some rabbinic commentators explain that these are the afflictions which purge man, and ultimately allow him to enter the World to Come, the rabbinic notion of an afterlife. This type of suffering is considered by the rabbis a gift from a loving and concerned God. But I wasn't quite sure how suffering alone, for the sake of suffering, can purge a person. It sounded a bit sadistic and it definitely didn't strike me as a Jewish concept.

But, once again, I was wrong. Rabbi Abraham Isaac Kook (1865–1935), the first Ashkenazi Chief Rabbi of Israel, explains how suffering can purge a person. He explained that "afflictions of love" serve to develop a person's spirituality in a way that even prayer and Torah learning cannot.

I admit that when I first heard this piece of Rabbi Kook's teachings, I didn't fully comprehend it. How could afflictions, which are beyond one's control, be in the same category as Torah and prayer, which are hard work (religiously speaking) in terms of building piety? Rabbi Carmy's analysis of Rabbi Soloveitchik – in addition to Frankl's work – shed some light on the matter.

When someone suffers physically or intellectually, it should be perceived as an invitation from God to step back and evaluate her relationship with Him. It isn't necessarily a punishment; it's a tap on the back. (Or in some cases, a slap on the backside of the head.) It is like a parent sending his child to his room to think. *It isn't meant to bring man down; it's meant to raise him up.* It's a signal from Someone Who Cares that He longs to reestablish a stronger relationship with you.

Now I had a new model to work with. I wasn't searching for a particular sin; I was seeking to re-evaluate my relationship with God. But how does one go about reevaluating a relationship? Perhaps the answer lies in the definition of "relationship."

CHAPTER EIGHTEEN

Redefining Yourself

MARTIN BUBER WAS what I liked to call a philosopher-poet. He had the mind of a philosopher but the soul of a poet. He was born in Vienna in 1878, but moved to Lemberg (which was then the capital of Austria, Galicia) at the age of three to live with his grandparents after his parents divorced. His grandfather was a Jewish scholar, and his grandmother a lover of German classics. They exposed Buber to both secular and religious studies as a child.

He returned to the home of his father in 1892, and at the ripe old age of fourteen began to read Kant and Nietzche. (What were you reading at fourteen?) It was then that he started to experience religious doubts. He abandoned the religious life of his grandparents and went to study in university. It might be fair to say that he abandoned his heart for his mind.

Buber was estranged from religion until he was introduced to Zionism, which brought him back to certain cultural aspects of Judaism. In 1904, he left the Zionist movement and went to live and study amongst Hassidim in Galicia. He was attracted to the joy and the emphasis on relationships that he found in Hassidism. But he did not become a Hassid. Instead, Buber left Galicia and became a professor of Jewish History in Frankfort.

After the rise of Nazi party, he left Germany and went to Israel, where he became a professor of sociology at Hebrew University in Jerusalem. But

Hassidism greatly influenced his thought, as a brief glance at a picture of him will tell you. His cottony beard and laughing eyes ultimately told the story of his soul. Buber loved people. People loved Buber. And Buber loved God.

In his book *I and Thou*, Buber claims that a person is defined by his relationships. There are two basic varieties of relationships: I–Thou, and I–It. In an I–It relationship, a person relates to another as a means rather than an ends. For example, if I am a student in a classroom, I might relate to the teacher as a means of gathering information. This isn't necessarily an inappropriate relationship. But when a teacher and a student maintain an exchange of ideas, when there is a mutuality in the relationship, when both the teacher and the student learn from each other and the teacher is no longer simply a means to an end, but an end in himself, an I–Thou relationship is formed. This I–Thou relationship is not characterized by the ideas that are exchanged between the teacher and the student or the benefit that one receives from the other. It is the unquantifiable essence of the relationship. It can't be expressed in words; it has to be experienced.

Buber brings the example of a tree. A tree can be perceived scientifically. It can be classified and studied. A very solid I–It relationship can be established with a tree. But a person can also develop a more meaningful relationship with the tree. He can nurture it and relate to it as a whole rather than a sum of its independent parts. Anyone who has ever taken care of a flowering plant, or raked the autumn leaves from under a flaming orange tree, can identify with this feeling. It is distinctly different from a scientific perspective. It is even more than an aesthetic appreciation. It is identifying yourself in relation to it. This is an I–Thou relationship.

Although it is natural to assume that relationships generally begin as I–It and evolve into I–Thou, the other direction is entirely possible, as well. Buber's example with the tree reminds me of Shel Silverstein's book, *The Giving Tree*. The book opens with an I–Thou relationship. The boy and the tree play together. They play *king of the forest* and the boy swings in the tree's branches and eats her apples and makes the tree "very happy." Both appreciate the other and partake in a mutual relationship. There is an inexplicable experience between the tree and the boy that you can sense when you read the book even though the author doesn't (and couldn't) spell it out. But as the book develops, the boy grows older, and the classic I–Thou relationship turns into an I–It relationship.

Eventually, the boy makes a boat from the tree's wood and sails away. The boy relates to the tree as a means rather than an ends in itself. But one of the most interesting parts of the book lies in the fact that the relationship between the tree and boy define who they are. The tree is never independent in the book. Neither is the boy. They are always viewed in relation to one another.

This is Buber's view of Man. Man is always identified by his relationships. There is no I. There is only an I–It and an I–Thou.

I remember lying in bed as a child and realizing for the first time that I was not one person. I was different people depending on whom I was with at the time. With my brothers, I was the annoying little tag-along who constantly got them into trouble; with my friends I was the boyish baseball freak; with my parents I was their cuddly baby girl; with my teachers I was the consummate student. I remember being utterly confused. Who was I really? (I was a deep kid.)

The funny thing was that I didn't get an answer until my early twenties, when I met my future husband. Here was someone I could be with, *without* acting out a role. I think it would be fair to say that I had finally developed a recognition of a unique I–Thou relationship. There was mutuality. We didn't perceive each other as means; we appreciated each other with no other strings attached. There was an essence to our relationship that defied categories and explanations. Buber might point out that it took my relationship with someone else to allow me to figure out who I was. Maybe it was our similarities. Maybe it was our differences. Maybe for the first time I was mature enough to recognize unconditional love. My older brother once told me that I changed after I met my would-be husband. He was wrong. I had changed for my brother. I had changed for my friends. I had changed for my parents. I had changed for my teachers. With my husband, I could finally stop changing.

But how does one go about establishing an I–Thou relationship with God? God gives us so many things – or we want Him to – that it seems that *by definition* we treat Him as a means rather than an ends. We need Him for everything! He gives us life, health, and wealth. How does one go about perceiving God as more than just a provider?

It struck me that *that* was the problem with the question of suffering. When we view God as a means to our happiness we feel jilted when we are afflicted with pain. We sense that God must be annoyed with us because he stopped performing His most basic function: rewarding our good behavior, or our lack of bad behavior, by fulfilling our wishes. This is what makes us ask the question: Why do good people suffer?

But the question is based on an I–It model. It's based on the assumption that God is a means to our happiness. If we perceived God differently, if we used an I–Thou model to form a new type of relationship, perhaps the question of suffering would fade away (or at least not jump out at us so impatiently.)

But, according to Buber, an I–Thou relationship with God is not something you can actively create. It finds you. You have to be receptive to it, and sit passively and wait. I can't think of a more difficult thing to do. Just open yourself up to the possibility, and then . . . just wait.

And what would an I–Thou relationship with God be like? How would it feel? I understood I–Thou between humans, because I have experienced it. Think of the first time you saw your newborn, or your wife-to-be. Or, even better, think of how you felt when your five-year-old walked through the front door after his first day of kindergarten. His face was smudged with mud, his hair was cut by his friend when the teacher wasn't looking, and his hands had some unidentified glowing green stuff stuck to it. But when he caught your eye and he ran into your open arms and the green stuff got on your new shirt, you really didn't care, did you? There are no words to describe that feeling, because words don't do it. That moment, you established an I–Thou relationship. You didn't actively seek it, by the way. It came running into your waiting arms.

An I–Thou relationship with God is similar. It's an unabashed, unscripted, unlimited appreciation for Him despite the glowing green stuff, or the smudged face, or the car accidents, or the disease, or the suffering that comes with it. And you can't actively seek it. But you do have to be open to it. And when you are, it hits you like a five-year-old running into your arms.

Buber's other point regarding relationships is even more interesting. Relationships, as we mentioned above, define you. There is no "I"; there is only an "I–Thou" or an "I–It." Relationships with God are no exception. Yet, prior to my accident, my relationship with God was defined by others. I had developed a religious persona based on what my teachers and parents taught me about God and what they said He expected of me. I had never conducted an independent study of God. *Who is God and what does He want from me? Why does He allow suffering in His world? What is the true nature of faith?* Using the wealth of philosophical and traditional texts I had at my disposal, coupled with my personal experience with suffering, it was finally time for me to come to my own conclusions.

CHAPTER NINETEEN

Who is God?

HOW CAN ONE describe God?

It is a common question in religious philosophy that is assumed under the topic of "Attributes." Namely, how can we attribute any adjectives to the Infinite? God is so *Other*; how can we use human language to describe Him? And yet if we can't describe Him, how can we relate to Him? Philosophers over the years have come up with all sorts of solutions.

One of the most accepted is the concept of "Attributes of Action." This is the idea that while we can't describe the essence of God, we can come to understand something about God by the way He acts. So, for example, if we see that someone who has been very sick is suddenly better, we can know that God acts in the ways of a healer. We can study the way God acts with humanity in order to get a better perspective on Him. The Torah is a good place to start because it is primarily concerned with God's relationship with mankind. I went to the first statement God is said to have made to man. Expecting to find a command, I was surprised that God's first statement to man was a blessing:

> *"Be fruitful and multiply and replenish the Earth, and subdue it, and have dominion over the fish of the sea and the fowl of the heaven . . . behold I have given you every herb yielding seed and every tree in which there is fruit yielding seed, for you it shall be food."* (Genesis 1:28)

Thus God introduces Himself to humanity: not as an authoritarian, not as a supreme, infinite leader, but as a Father who has prepared a wondrous home for His children to live in and whose greatest desire is to bless His firstborn. When we first encounter God, we find love, just as when a newborn first encounters his mother. It's an overwhelming love. It's a head swimming, dizzying kind of love. It makes us want to give that baby everything we have and then some. Which is exactly what God does.

The second time God speaks to man He gives him a command:

> *"Of every tree of the garden thou mayest freely eat, but of the tree of knowledge of good and evil thou shalt not eat of it; for in the day that thou eatest thereof, thou shalt surely die."*   (Genesis 2:16, 17)

It was a strange command. What was this 'tree of knowledge of good and evil,' and why was it associated with death? The question deepens when one reads on in the familiar story of The Fall. The snake tries to convince Eve to eat from the tree by claiming that it will make her and her mate "like God." How would eating this fruit make man like God?

Commentators and scholars have struggled with this story for centuries. Christianity bases some of its central doctrines on this puzzling tale. But every time I read it, I felt like I was missing something. There must be some powerful truth behind it, but what did it mean? Just recently, I read an interpretation that I think really captures the message. The story of Adam's sin is a story about the basis of morality.

Is morality objective, or is it based on an individual's relative assessment? The question gnaws at the very core of religion when it morphs into, *Do we need God in order to be moral? Or can we figure out a clear system of morality based on our own instincts, intuitions, or intellects?*

Philosophers have developed independent systems of morality, the most famous being Kant's *categorical imperative*: Kant posits that one should only act according to a rule that he would wish to become universal. In other words, I should only do what I would wish to see everyone else do. If I see an older woman struggling with her packages, I should help her. That is a rule that can be universalized quite nicely. We would clearly wish for all mankind to act in this way. Kant's system is certainly intuitive, but is it enough? Kant's own example might help us decide: someone is fleeing from a murderer and he tells you that he is going home to hide. Then the murderer himself approaches you and asks the whereabouts of this individual. Should you lie? It seems obvious that you should not tell this murderer where his potential victim is hiding. You *should* lie. Tell him he's at the library.

But Kant's categorical imperative would instead have you ask the question, Would I like lying to become a universally acceptable act? The answer of course is no, so you cannot lie to the murderer. Kant justifies this rather odd conclusion by explaining that we really never know the consequences of our actions. Perhaps, if I lie and tell the murderer that the potential victim is not in his house, but in the library, and the victim, on a whim, in fact chooses to go to the library to catch up on some light reading, the murderer would run into him there (having been an avid reader himself) and kill him. According to Kant, we never really know the consequences of our actions, so we should always adhere to unmoving universal principles like 'no lying.'

What Kant clearly has not taken into account is that sometimes we really can predict with fair certainty the results of our actions. The guy running away probably ran to his house if that is what he told you he would do. By lying, you can be fairly certain of saving this person's life. Another thing Kant's system fails to consider is what happens when there are two conflicting universal values at play. In the above example, the value of preserving human life is threatened by the value of being truthful. How do you know which value to uphold?

There are other philosophical moral theories. Natural Law adherents like St. Thomas Aquinas propose that the laws of morality are inherent in our reason. Namely, if left to our own devices, man could and would come up with a perfectly moral society. I can't argue with the notion of basic moral instincts, but as Rabbi Soloveitchik points out (in *Reflections of the Rav*), a person often needs an external impetus to follow these basic moral laws. How often have we talked ourselves into believing that we are doing the right thing, despite the fact that we are clearly doing the wrong thing? It is all too easy to rationalize our actions, even if they are clearly wrong to others (or even to ourselves in moments of clarity). There needs to be a Divine figure, God, who commands us to act in moral ways – to give us that extra push, to take away our ability to rationalize ourselves into acting incorrectly.

For example, there is a law in the Torah that if someone is walking on a road and he passes a person whose donkey has fallen, he should help this person. This law – predating the Good Samaritan parable by a few centuries, and the social psychology models thereof by two millennia – seems so obvious, and yet . . . . How easy it would be to reason our way out of helping him: "I don't even know him; maybe he's a thief"; "I'm in a bit of rush; I'll help him on my way back if he's still there"; "That donkey is way too heavy and I threw out my back last week." The Torah takes these excuses out of the picture. There is a requirement to help this guy, so get off of your high horse (literally) and help him!

The answer to the question of the basis for morality is dealt with in the Torah in the story of Adam and Eve's sin. God instructs man that He is the only basis of morality – not man. He tells Adam, Do what you want with any of the other trees, but don't eat from *that* one! By obeying God's command, Adam would have acknowledged that God is the ultimate Decider of right and wrong. Quite simply, that He knows more than we do in the realm of goodness. God has the ability to make the appropriate decisions when there is a conflict of values, or when things seem to be morally ambiguous. And by having Him as the ultimate Decider, we can't talk ourselves out of correct moral positions.

By disobeying the command, Adam attempted to become the arbiter of good and evil himself (hence the name of the tree), God-like (as the snake suggested), and morality, therefore, becomes relative.

It is one general purpose of religion to provide morality based on an objective system decided by God; otherwise, things can go very wrong. The Torah warns of death and destruction to man should he start trying to become the judge of morality from a Godless place. And the Torah has proved itself to be right; slavery was deemed moral in the South in the 1800s; Communism claimed the lives of over 100 million people in the name of the "greater good"; and it was perfectly moral to torture and gas 11 million men, women, and children in Nazi Germany toward the perfection of the Aryan race.

Thus, as understood by the Bible, after God establishes Himself as the Creator (and loving Parent to His creations), He also establishes Himself as the One Who decides right from wrong. God alone is the arbiter of justice in the world. It's significant that the very issue that brought me to this inquiry (God's justice) is also one of the first issues the Torah deals with. Clearly, the question of good and evil plays a big role in this universe on many levels. But that isn't the only thing the Torah has to say about God and His relationship with His creations. God is perceived in roles other than judge and jury in the stories that follow the saga of Adam and Eve in the Garden of Eden.

CHAPTER TWENTY

Ten Tests

THERE IS A rabbinic tradition that Abraham was tested by God no less than ten times (Mishna Avot 5:3). The lists of the ten tests vary, but according to Maimonides, the first test occurred almost immediately after we are introduced to Abraham. Here's the backstory: We are told that a man named Terah from Ur of the Chaldees had three sons: Abram, Nahor, and Haran. Haran died in Ur and Terah took the rest of his family to Haran, where he died at the age of 250.

The very next chapter marks the beginning of Abraham's prominent career as forefather of a nation. God speaks to Abraham and tells him to leave his father's home and to go to the land that He will show him. God promises Abraham that He will make him into a great nation, his name will be well-known, and he will be a source of blessing for the world. So just like that, taking God at His word, Abraham ups and leaves prosperity and family in Haran for an unknown desert, at the age of seventy-five. This was not retirement; it was starting over like a college student. The stories of his various travels make up the rest of the chapter.

This was considered Abraham's first test. But the biblical narrative seems to have left out some pertinent information. Why did God single out Abraham? What had Abraham done in his life to make God think that he was "the one?" And why was he required to leave his father's homeland? Couldn't he have

performed his function in Haran? The Midrash (Oral Tradition) fills in some
of these details:

> The Lord said to Abraham, "Leave your land, your birthplace, and
> your father's house . . ." To what may this be compared? To a man
> who was traveling from place to place when he saw a palace in flames
> (*alternate translation*: a palace full of light). He wondered, "Is it pos-
> sible that the palace lacks an owner?" The owner of the palace looked
> out and said, "I am the owner of the palace." So it was that Abraham
> our father said, "Is it possible that the world lacks a ruler?" The Holy
> One . . . looked out and said to him, "I am the ruler, the Sovereign of
> the universe." (Bereshit Rabbah 39:1)

The Midrash supplies us with a hint as to what was going on with Abraham
prior to his first recorded (and dramatic) encounter with God, in which he
was told to leave his father's home. Abraham saw a "palace in flames" or a
"palace full of light." What was this palace, and why does he claim that it must
have an owner?

When I first read this midrash I assumed that the "palace full of light" was
a metaphor for the universe. Abraham beheld the magnificent universe and
claimed that an intricate, complex, wondrous place like this couldn't have occurred by accident. It must have a designer. This line of logic is one of the classical proofs for the existence of God. It is called the "argument from design"
and it has a long philosophical history that officially stems back to the Greeks.
But according to this Midrash, the argument was even older. Abraham discovered it on his own and it led him to become the father of monotheism.

But Jonathan Sacks, chief rabbi of Britain, offers a vastly different interpretation in his book *Radical Then, Radical Now* (a must-read!). Rabbi Sacks
argues that the correct reading of the Midrash entails Abraham seeing a palace consumed by flames, and not a palace full of light. The palace is still a
metaphor for the well-ordered universe, but it is consumed by the flames of
disorder and injustice. Abraham sees this palace on fire and asks, where is the
owner of this palace? Why doesn't he put out the flames? Abraham is bothered by the question of suffering and evil in the world. He sees a beautiful,

harmonious universe being perverted and disrupted by evil, and he wonders why nobody is doing anything to stop it. Where is the owner? Why can't he do anything? It is the cry of the sufferer. It is the cry of the victim. It is the cry that sparked monotheism.

God answered the cry by identifying Himself as the Owner. But that's all he offered to Abraham. He didn't supply a detailed plan of how he would end suffering in this world. He didn't claim to be the cause of the suffering. The cause of the flames was not the owner of the palace, it was its inhabitants. People cause the evils in this world, because God decided to give them free will. But now that they have this power of choice, God is "powerless" to stop them. His only option would be to take away their freedom – and wouldn't that be an evil in itself? So God is silent. Only people can put out the flames that they have ignited. And that became Abraham's task, writes Sacks.

God recognized Abraham because Abraham recognized God. Abraham saw that the world had a Creator. But that wasn't all. God chose Abraham because Abraham recognized the injustice of the world and had a desire to fix it. God found a partner in Abraham. Together they would spread the message of monotheism and justice to the rest of humanity. Abraham's first test was designed to set him on his destined path.

But couldn't Abraham have spread this message at home in Haran? Surely the people there would have benefited from it; they were the ones that had upset Abraham with their iniquity in the first place!

Abraham needed a new start. While he was in his father's house, he still perceived himself as part of his father's clan. To be the founder of a brand new concept, you need to make a clean break. Abraham had to begin perceiving himself not as his father's son, but as a separate innovative force with something unique to contribute. He needed to acquire a degree of independence from his past.

Abraham's role would not be an easy one. He lived in a time in which mankind's notion of a deity was housed in a stone statue. Abraham's beliefs were considered radical and outside the confines of accepted religion. People of his time called him "*Ivri*" or "Other." He was singled out. He was segregated. Often, he was treated differently. The entire world stood on one side and Abraham would have to stand squarely on the other. Leaving his home would be Abraham's first step in his training program. And God would be his Coach.

The rest of the ten trials served the same purpose as the first. They served to prepare Abraham for the tasks that lay ahead of him; to enable him to properly fulfill those jobs. His wife was taken away from him . . . twice; his nephew was kidnapped, requiring him to fight the armies of four kings to rescue him; he was commanded to circumcise himself at the age of ninety-nine; and he was promised a son with Sarah, but in desperation, married her handmaid, Hagar, because no child was forthcoming. His life was by all accounts difficult, but these events played crucial roles in developing his character.

Sarah was taken away from him when Abraham demonstrated that he lacked the proper perspective on her role in their mission. Sarah was his partner. We are told that Abraham taught the men about God and Sarah taught the women. They shared the responsibility of spreading monotheism. But when they reached Egypt, Abraham lied. He told the Egyptians that Sarah was his sister because he feared for his life – he thought that on account of her great beauty the locals would kill him in order to take her.

But the lie demonstrated a problem in Abraham's judgment. He didn't properly value her contribution to his cause; she was more than just a pretty face – she was half the operation. So Sarah was taken away from him. It was only in her absence that he began to perceive her as an equal partner in their mission. God tested Abraham to teach him this lesson. God wasn't punishing him; God was teaching him. God was his Mentor. And He employed life events to inculcate His lessons. But the most heart-wrenching test by far was the last one: the tenth test.

The one thing Abraham had wished most for in life was a child. God promised him that he would have a son who would inherit the Land He gave Abraham. But it was more than that. Abraham wanted a son to inherit his beliefs and his values to which he dedicated his life. Ishmael did not quite fit the bill. Abraham was not sure that this child was indeed his spiritual heir, and more than that: he was not borne of his true partner, Sarah.

But one hundred years into his life, God finally granted him an heir for his kingdom of ideas. It was the one reward Abraham really sought. He would lavish everything on Isaac. He would teach him everything he had come to discover about God and this new religion. Finally, someone to pass on his hard-earned knowledge to. But then God tells him to do a disturbing thing:

> *"Take your son, your only son, whom you love, Isaac, and go to the land of Moriah, and bring him as an offering on one of the mountains which I will show you."* (Genesis 22:2)

It is difficult to imagine what was going through Abraham's mind when he heard those words. God had asked him to kill his one dream in life – his son. He spent a century longing for a child, and in one swift blow he was being asked – commanded – to give him up. But it was more than that: Abraham was the founder of a new religion. He ushered in new ideas about God and the proper way of serving Him. Idolaters brought their children as offerings: not Abraham. It was against all of his religious principles. It was against his very conception of God! With this one command, God had him questioning his whole life's work.

But the Torah narrative doesn't relate any of this. It simply relates what Abraham did: He woke up early, saddled his donkey, and brought Isaac to Mount Moriah.

On his trip up the mountain, Isaac turns to his father and asks, "Here is the wood, but where is the lamb for the offering?" Abraham responds, "God will give us the lamb, my son" (Genesis 22:7–8). How painful it must have been for Abraham to say those words, knowing that his tender son *was* the lamb!

Once he reaches the appointed place, Abraham sets up his offering. But just as he is about to kill his son, an angel from heaven cries:

> *"Abraham, Abraham . . . lay not thy hand upon the lad . . . for now I know that thou art a God-fearing man, seeing that thou hast not withheld thy son, thine only son, from Me."* (Genesis, 22: 12,13)

Looking up, Abraham sees a ram caught in a thorn bush. That ram would replace his son as the offering. The angel spoke once again. He explained that now that Abraham's fear of God had been proven, God would multiply his children to be like the stars in the sky and the sand on the beach. And He would bless them . . . . And then Abraham returned home to Be'er Sheva. That's all we are told about the end of this trauma.

Abraham must have been exhausted – emotionally, physically, spiritually – when this ordeal was over. Maybe he tried to get it out of his head. Or maybe he understood the meaning of the test, and was proud to have reached this milestone of religious fervor. The narrative doesn't tell us. It leaves it to the reader to speculate.

But what did the test mean, and what purpose could it possibly have been meant to serve? Why would God do this to his most faithful servant? How could God risk a test like this? Morally, it seems like just the kind of thing that Abraham's God would *not* want to command.

The way I see it, the test served two very important functions. Firstly, it was a test for *Abraham* – a personality inventory as it were, for him to better know himself. Tests administered by God are not for God to see how well the person performs. God knows how the person will perform. Tests administered by God are for the person to see how well they can perform.

Abraham probably never imagined that he would be able to sacrifice his son. But that knowledge was holding him back from achieving something. It was only during the test that Abraham grew into the kind of person who would be willing to sacrifice his most beloved "possession" to God. But then something important happened. God told him to stop. God told him that now that he had achieved the heights of religious devotion, he had to know that God would *never* truly ask him to carry it out.

God had to very publicly teach Abraham, and the world, that Judaism was unique, different from all of the other religions in the ancient world. Judaism didn't – and doesn't – value death for God as much as it values life for God.

As such, the story of the binding of Isaac served two purposes. It served to teach Abraham about his own devotion. But it also taught the world what to do with that religious devotion. In the days of Abraham, people were misguided. They thought killing their most prized assets, their children (who were considered possessions in those days, long before society began to recognize children as individuals), was the ultimate level in serving their respective deities. God was teaching them, in a most dramatic way, that they were wrong.

Living a life of religious fervor is better than *dying* for religious fervor. Thus, God blessed Abraham with children and more children and more children.

Life as devotion: It was a radical new theory of religion. (And it is a message that is uniquely suited to our times, as well.) What started as the worst type of mental suffering that God could inflict on man is now understood as a powerful didactic tool. It allowed Abraham to activate his own potential, and it taught the world a critical lesson. Thus, in the ten tests of Abraham, God stars in a new role: as Teacher or Mentor.

The stories of Abraham's tests are not just the personal memoirs of one man. They are recorded in the Torah to teach humanity something new. They provide us with an insight into the relationship between ourselves and God. Earlier, we saw Him as the ultimate Decider of morality. He was viewed as a distant judge – a supreme court judge, perhaps, rather than a judge of a lower civil court. But with the story of Abraham, we see a God who works closely with individuals to enable them to develop spiritually, emotionally, and intellectually so that they can fulfill their goals. God is not just a distant judge; He is a Homeroom Teacher (the good ones, not the fourth grade ones who suspend you for something you didn't do . . . . Sorry I can't seem to let go of that one).

God is the Coach you want your seventh grade son to have. He's the Art Teacher you want you third grade daughter to get. He's the Tutor you want your child with special needs to study with. He works with each individual to cultivate his or her talents. Some lessons are tougher than others; but they all come from the right place.

CHAPTER TWENTY-ONE

A Scalding Hot Cup of Coffee

THE ACCIDENT HAD proved to be about a lot of things. I began to understand myself and my need to allow my intellect to share space with other
things. I gained a new perspective on my complex relationship with God. But
perhaps most importantly, I started to redefine my concept of faith.

The limits of the human intellect are a difficult pill to swallow for most
academics. I remember reading an interview once that appeared in *Biblical
Archeology Review*. It was an article about how scholarship affected faith. The
group of scholars who were interviewed included an expert on the apocryphal
gospels who had lost his faith due to his scholarship; an archaeologist who was
a Baptist minister; a Dead Sea Scroll scholar who was an Orthodox Jew; and
another archaeologist who had also lost his faith.

The first scholar, the expert on the apocryphal gospels, explained that he
had first lost his fundamentalist beliefs when he'd found certain contradictions in the Bible, but had completely lost his faith when he taught a course
in theodicy.

He explained that he couldn't find any answers to the question of suffering that satisfied him, and he had no interest in believing in a God that had
anything to do with the terrible state of things in this world. I found it fascinating that the very thing that brought me to a deeper understanding of my
relationship with God brought him to deny God's existence.

I realized that our disagreement stems from different perspectives on the nature of faith. This scholar, like most in the Western world, believes that faith should provide consolation. It should provide answers and security. Like a warm cup of tea on a freezing winter day, faith is supposed to warm the soul. In Traditional Judaism, faith is perceived very differently. Historically, Jews have been called upon to proclaim their faith in times of persecution, rampage, and death. And historically, Jewish faith has strengthened despite (and often in the wake of) the questions that inevitably arose from intense suffering. In Judaism, faith isn't a comforting cup of tea; it is a scalding hot cup of coffee.

Elie Wiesel tells a story that elucidates the Jewish relationship to faith. In Auschwitz, Wiesel had befriended a teacher of Talmud who suggested they study Talmud together as an act of defiance. One night, this teacher took him by the arm and led him to his barracks where three scholarly rabbis waited. They had set up a rabbinic court where they intended to put God on trial.

The trial lasted a few nights. They called witnesses, gathered evidence, and in the end they came up with their verdict – God was guilty of crimes against humanity. An "infinity of silence" followed the verdict, relates Wiesel, only to be broken by his teacher, who looked up at the sky and declared, "It's time for *maariv,* the evening service." And the members of the court commenced the recitation of the evening prayers.

Complaining to God, complaining about God, even indicting him in a rabbinic court, was an acceptable Jewish response to the Holocaust, as long as it didn't lead to a *rejection* of God.

As long as one's basic commitment to God remains intact, one is free to explore his or her feelings and opinions about suffering. It is encouraged. It is an acknowledgment that faith had been challenged, and is indeed challenging. It is the sign of a thinking person, to question, even to rail against Heaven; faith does not come with the simple answers of simple people. The key is that despite it all, faith is never relinquished. Wiesel writes in his Memoir, *All Rivers Run into the Sea*:

> I have never renounced my faith in God. I have risen against His justice, protested His silence, and sometimes His absence, but my anger rises up within faith and not outside it . . . . Abraham and Moses,

Jeremiah and Rebbe Levi-Yitzhak of Berdichev teach us that it is permissible for man to accuse God, provided it is done in the name of faith in God. If that hurts, so be it. Sometimes we must accept the pain of faith so as not to lose it.

Therein lay the difference between my position (if I may jump onto Weisel's esteemed bandwagon) and that of the formerly fundamentalist scholar quoted in *Biblical Archeology Review*. The Bible scholar demanded things of his faith. He wanted faith to explain God's role in suffering. He wanted his faith to wash away his questions. He wanted his faith to become knowledge. I, however, came to realize that faith and knowledge were two completely different things. It is not the job of faith to answer questions that couldn't be answered. As a Jew, I am expected to have faith despite my questions. While this scholar sought things from *his* faith, *my* faith sought things from *me*.

What's more, I learned that due to its very nature, faith couldn't be based on knowledge. Kierkegaard, the 19th century Danish philosopher, considered to be the father of existentialism, once wrote:

> Faith is an absurdity. Its object is utterly unlikely, irrational, and beyond the reach of any argument . . . . Suppose someone decides that he wants to acquire faith. Let's follow this comedy. He wants to have faith, but at the same time he also wants to reassure himself that he is taking the right step – so he undertakes an objective inquiry into the probability that he is right. And what happens? By means of his objective inquiry into probability, the absurd becomes something different: it becomes probable . . . it becomes extremely and utterly probable. Now this person is ready to believe, and he tells himself that he doesn't believe in the way of ordinary men like shoemakers and tailors, but only after having thought the whole matter through properly and understood its probability. Now he is ready to believe. But lo and behold, at this very moment it becomes impossible for him to believe. Anything that is almost probable . . . or extremely and utterly probable, is something he can almost know . . . or extremely and utterly nearly know – but it is impossible to believe. For the absurd is the

object of faith, and the only object that can be believed. (Concluding unscientific postscript)

Kierkegaard asserted that faith cannot be knowledge and knowledge cannot be faith. The two are mutually exclusive. Once you prove that God existed, you could no longer believe it. That is why the philosophical proofs for the existence of God contribute nothing to religion. They might be able prove that God exists (depending on who you ask), but that leaves no room for faith. That was also why we cannot understand things like theodicy. The instant you understand it philosophically, it no longer lies in the realm of faith. And make no mistake about it: the true home for questions about God's existence and his tolerance of evil is in faith.

The more I understood about faith, the more I appreciated the differences between faith and knowledge. Faith is a welcoming ocean, while knowledge is an untouchable sky. Faith is a relationship with all of its insecurities, love, and companionship; knowledge is a library, a lab. Faith is a passionate lover; knowledge is old, wise – and sterile.

Religion should never become old, or sterile.

It's not that faith doesn't provide answers to life's "big questions"; it just doesn't provide *simple* answers, and it doesn't provide intellectual *certitude* for those answers. In other words, often the answers could not be proven by reason. This does not make the answers incorrect. It merely testifies to the fact that this universe is far too complex to be explained by logic alone.

The twentieth-century American philosopher, William James, once wrote, "Objective evidence and certitude are doubtless very fine ideals to play with, but where on this moonlit and dream-visited planet are they found?" (*The Will to Believe*). For James, a person could never be certain that he had arrived at Truth. It was a fact demonstrated by the multitudes of philosophical and scientific schools of thought that had purported to have discovered Truth, only to later be overturned by another equally convincing school of thought. James felt that the truth of an idea was judged by its outcome. *Did the idea enhance life?* If so, its "cash-value" made it true.

This notion is well demonstrated with the discussion of the origin of the universe. When Edwin Hubble discovered evidence that the universe was expanding, the Big Bang theory was born. The Big Bang theory posits that the universe arose from one huge explosion. The explosion originated from a singularity – sort of like a black hole – into which all the primordial "stuff" was squashed. With that explosion both space and time were born. What preceded and caused that explosion? It would clearly require something that pre-existed space and time. It would also call for something that is endowed with infinite energy. The conditions had to be perfect for this Big Bang to occur. Scientists can recount those conditions. They can even recreate the seconds following the Big Bang. But the question of what came before, or even what happened at that exact instant remains unanswered. Scientists have faith that mathematics and physics will one day be able to account for the Big Bang. Theists have faith that they already know the answer. One thing is abundantly clear – they all rely on faith of one sort or another.

Now we are faced with a conundrum. Should we have faith in science or God? Here is where James's point fits in nicely. James would say that because we can't be absolutely certain which position is right we must ask, What is the relative value of each position?

The scientific position stipulates an impersonal natural force (with some unpronounceable scientific name, no doubt) that caused an explosion beyond proportion and by chance formed a universe that supports intelligent life. Neither the force of nature nor the mathematical equation that describes the explosion would impose moral obligations upon human kind. They would not demand that man create just societies or forge meaningful relationships. They would not require man to better himself. They wouldn't really speak to man at all. Would they represent Truth though? One astronomer explains that the probability that a world as complex and finely tuned as ours could have been formed by chance may be likened to the probability that monkeys placed before typewriters would eventually create works of Shakespeare. The scientific version of the origin of the universe ultimately relies on the belief that these highly unlikely scenarios are still mathematically possible, making James's point even more poignant: intellectual Truth will always be elusive so we need to utilize a different standard.

The religious position involves faith in God. It is not any God. It is a personal God. One who does impose moral obligations. One Who commands mankind to act justly and with kindness toward one another. One Who espouses the ideals of peace, love, and devotion. One Who prods the individual to work on himself. So which truth has greater value – science or God?

I'm not implying that science doesn't contribute to society. I'm arguing that it doesn't necessarily contribute to the *fabric* of society. It doesn't add to the values or the goals through which society is formed. And while science and technology contribute great things to the advancement of a certain aspect of society, it doesn't really touch the heart of it, does it? It provides us with technology and intellectual understanding of the way things work. It provides us with medicines, and diagnostic devices. But what does it do for our collective and individual souls? *Does it make us better people?*

Letting go of our intellectual impulses is not a simple thing to do. Science and logic seem more true to us somehow than religious and intuitive truths. A recent book entitled *My Stroke of Insight* by Jill Bolte Taylor addresses this issue. Bolte Taylor is a brain scientist who suffered a stroke which left her bereft of her ability to talk, walk, read, write, and process information. The left hemisphere of her brain, which is responsible for processing sensory data, had deteriorated. The constant "brain chatter" – that logical voice in you head that accompanies you throughout your day reminding you to separate the laundry and buy pasta for dinner – was completely silenced. But surprisingly, Bolte Taylor describes the state she was in as "nirvana." For the first time in her life she experienced complete peace. She viewed the world exclusively through her right hemisphere which sees things in pictures rather than language. The right hemisphere experiences the Moment, before our left hemispheres begins to understand that moment in relation to the past and the future. The right hemisphere creates an image of the Moment replete with its smells, tastes, sights, and feelings. It is responsible for intuition, creativity and imagination. Bolte Taylor vividly describes how the atoms of her body appeared to merge with the atoms of the air surrounding her compelling her to view herself as being one with the universe. She explains that this unusual perspective is the purview of the right hemisphere and is what allows humans to experience empathy for others. Bolte Taylor's message to the world is that if at times we would all willingly step out of our left brains, whose job it is to make us distinct from the rest of humanity, we could all achieve peace and project it into the world. She suggests listening to music, practicing yoga, meditating, and praying as possible methods of attaining this unique perspective.

The right and the left brain think differently and they have two very different messages for us. Science, with its distinctions and categories, lies squarely in the left hemisphere; while faith, with its messages of beauty, peace and unity, rests comfortably in the right. And the logic of the left brain is not more important or truthful than the experiences of the right. They are both aspects of who we are.

Lawrence Schiffman, the Orthodox Jewish scholar in the *Biblical Archeology Review* interview, made another crucial point about the nature of faith. He said, "I see the whole thing as a lifelong quest. It's not either a person believes or doesn't believe. The life experiences of people are very different and very complex, and believing in God is itself a challenge.... Faith is a process."

I had never before thought of faith as a process, but once I read this statement I felt like I had arrived at something I had been searching for since the beginning of my philosophical journey. The fact is, faith *is* a process. It is not something someone is born with and carries with him through his life – status unchanged. Man goes through life, encounters different challenges, and is expected to respond to them. Sometimes his response is to uphold his original faith, sometimes he reevaluates his faith and even redefines it, and sometimes he briefly abandons it altogether.

The point is that faith is a process, just like life. It isn't a name you take on at birth; it is more like your body that keeps changing and growing with you. When faith is perceived as a process rather than a 'yes' or 'no' answer, one can begin to recognize stages and degrees of faith. Faith becomes a complex state of mind rather than blind acceptance. A deeper faith is one that has been challenged.

This is what is meant by the rabbinic claim that 'One who had sinned and repented is greater than one who has never sinned.' It is the challenge to faith that causes it to become more sophisticated. It is the challenge to faith that lends it more depth.

I was finally at a stage in my religious recovery where I could not only embrace the accident, but I could even embrace the religious skepticism that preceded it.

There was yet another important facet of faith that I was coming to appreciate as I went through my own "process": Faith could only be acquired by the single individual, alone. Nobody could teach it to you. Nobody could preach it to you. It could not be replicated from somebody else. It had to come from deep within a person. And it often came after years of treacherous soul searching. The only things that could be compared to the intensity of a faith crisis are extreme joy, or extreme sadness. (Both, incidentally, are also components of religious crisis.)

The seventeenth-century French philosopher, Blaise Pascal, metaphorically described the choice to believe as "a flip of the coin." The argument came to be known as *Pascal's Wager*. Suppose, he said, that you had to choose between believing in God, or not. Human reason provided no clues, so a game might be played in your head – Heads, I believe, or Tails, I don't. How to decide which to call? You must weigh what you would gain by each of the choices. If you choose Heads (to believe in God), and there indeed *is* a God, you might gain "eternal beatitude." If you chose Heads and there is *no* God, you lose nothing. What is the consequence, after all, of a bet with yourself?

There is only one losing wager: choosing Tails (denying God) when there is a God, in which case you stand to be "condemned to eternal damnation." By choosing to believe, then, you either win, or lose nothing. On the other hand, by choosing not to believe, you could lose in a very profound way.

It is an interesting thought experiment, but ultimately, it couldn't work to convince someone to believe. Put simply – you can't just *tell* someone to believe. William James points out that you can't even convince them intellectually that they stand to gain from believing. A person has to have the desire to believe in order to be able to truly believe.

Belief is not something you can even tell *yourself* to do. It is something you have to feel deep within your gut. It is something that you have to intuit. It is like love. Nobody can convince you to love someone else. People can try – extolling the virtues of the person in question, pointing to his grey eyes, his strong chin, or his generous nature. But ultimately, love is something that has to come from deep within your gut. It can't be taught. It can't be lectured. It can't be quantified or intellectualized. Often it can't even be explained! Like love, faith is something a person has to experience.

CHAPTER TWENTY-TWO

Grazing the Fingertips of God

THERE IS A myriad of reasons for people to lose faith. Some have intellectual doubts, others have experienced tragedy, and some just can't seem to sense what others sense in the spiritual realm. And yet the Torah has high expectations. We are commanded to love and fear God. We are told by Maimonides that the "foundation of foundations" is to know there is a God. But how can we know there is a God when He is so maddeningly elusive?

Abraham Joshua Heschel (1907–1972) dedicates his book *God in Search of Man* to this question. He explains that there are three ways for man to approach God: by sensing his presence in the world, by sensing his presence in the Torah, and by sensing his presence in deeds.

In describing the first method (sensing God's presence in the world) Heschel explains the basic problem with modern man. Modern man refuses to see the wonder and the mystery of the universe: "The Greeks learned in order to comprehend. The Hebrews learned in order to revere. The modern man learns in order to use." Modern man is convinced that nature is there is serve him. He studies nature so that he can manipulate it for his own needs. Modern education has suffered from the same phenomenon. We teach children how to count, and measure, but we fail to teach them how to wonder. We have taken the mystery out of the universe, and we have lost our souls in the process.

Reading Heschel's words reminded me of one morning I spent in Jerusalem as a young adult. I had woken up early – before sunrise, in fact – and slipped out of bed quietly. I didn't want to wake my parents. We had been visiting my brother in Jerusalem, but that morning would be our last one in Israel. We were returning to the States that day.

I rubbed my back (the pull-out couch was small and wiry) and tiptoed toward my clothes that were flung over a nearby chair. I silently got dressed and made my escape. I had a destination, I just didn't know it yet. I started to walk around and noted how the neighborhood had changed in the last five years. I had gone to school in the same neighborhood the year after high school, but the area was markedly different. The suburb-within-a-city of Bayit Vegan is situated on a hill. When I had studied there, the hill was not completely developed. My college lay toward the bottom of the hill, and a road circled its way up to the next street which was located in the middle of the incline. If you didn't want to walk all the way around, you could climb your way over the rocks, sand, and broken shards of concrete toward some half-built steps that would lead you to the next block. But now, a short five years later, the whole hill was developed. I could skip my way up on a finished stone staircase, passing charming houses, green yards, and tiled terraces along the way. I started to make my way up the hill, still unsure of where I was going.

The sun had just started to rise, but I couldn't see it yet. I noticed that the black sky had turned a light brown. It was an eerie color. I felt like I was looking at an old picture of a town from the 1800s. I kept climbing my way up the stairs, noting the solidity of the Jerusalem stone beneath my feet. It wasn't sand and rocks anymore, it was slabs of stone. I reached a terrace to an elegant little house and stopped to rest on a ledge. I looked out at the sky and was pleased to catch the first hint of the sun's ascent. It was rising very slowly, I thought to myself. It was almost as if the sun knew I was waiting for it, and had decided to play some cruel game with me. I knew it had to show its face eventually, and I was starting to feel my exhaustion, so I just sat and waited.

The sun was a dull orange at its smallest. I remember thinking that there should have been more colors to this sunrise, but there was just orange. I was soon to discover that the magic wasn't in the variety of colors, it was in the variant shades of orange. I never knew there could be so many versions of the same color. It started with a mixture of orange and gray, but slowly the gray veil dissipated, revealing the different stages of the color: at first there were shades of rusty, burnt orange, which morphed into more citrusy hues, and then took on a bright amber color. At its height it became florescent: a gleaming Orange Sapphire adorning the early morning sky.

That's when I pulled out my prayer book. I had slipped it into my pocket before I left my room, thinking that I might choose to say morning prayers if I found the right spot. I had found it.

Heschel's modern man might have said that I simply observed the effects of the gas molecules in the atmosphere. Apparently, the orange colors of the sun at sunrise derive from the fact that the rays of the light spectrum have a difficult time passing through the thick molecules in our atmosphere. Only the yellow, orange, and red rays can get through because they have longest wavelengths. But surely, this man would have been missing the point. I didn't observe wavelengths; I observed magic. That magic is the source of faith.

Maimonides makes a similar point to Heschel's. In the second chapter of *The Laws of the Foundations of the Torah*, Maimonides asks: How can one inspire himself to love and fear God? His answer is deceptively simple. He claims that when man sits and contemplates nature and its inherent and infinite wisdom, he will immediately praise, and long to understand, God. On the face of it, this is strikingly similar to the well-known argument from Intelligent Design: Man sees that the world was created with a uniquely inspired design, so he must conclude that it has a designer.

But Maimonides is speaking about *love* of God in this section, not knowledge of His existence. And Maimonides describes a longing for God. He wasn't referring to a philosophical argument. He must have meant something akin to what I experienced on that ledge in Bayit Vegan.

When man is exposed to the symphonic beauty of the universe, he is overwhelmed by the harmony and sheer radiance of it. His brain will probably leap to the conclusion that the world could not be a random accident. But that intellectual leap is not faith. Later, that same man will come up with counters to his original intellectual reaction. It is the moment *before* he makes that cognitive jump that is the moment of faith; *that* is the indisputable moment that inspires love. It is the inexplicable sense of awe that overpowers him. It is the exquisite instant of pure entrancement. It is the sudden encounter with consummate perfection. It is the intuitive moment that points to the infinite.

Modern man's failure to notice the wonder in the world stems from the fact that he truly believes that all of the mysteries of the universe will one day be placed under the rubric of science, and there will be no need to resort to God for explanations. It's an interesting claim. But when one considers that Galileo Galilei, Johannes Kepler, Isaac Newton, Robert Boyle, Gottfried Liebnitz, William Thomson Kelvin, and Max Planck all believed in a personal God, one might hesitate to make such a claim. Furthermore, scientists have failed thus far to come up with a proven unified theory to explain the way the universe functions. And, as Stephen Hawking points out in his conclusion of *A Brief History of Time*:

> Even if there is only one possible unified theory, it is just a set of rules and equations. What is it that breathes fire into the equations and makes a universe for them to describe? . . . Why does the universe go to all the bother of existing? Is the unified theory so compelling that it brings about its own existence? Or does it need a creator, and if so, does he have any other effect on the universe? And who created him?

Science only explains observed phenomena, it doesn't ask or answer the question, Why? Hawking laments the fact that science and philosophy have been to reduced to dealing with smaller issues. But the truth is, science has grasped all it can fit into its tiny fists. The grander questions are by definition unanswerable from a scientific point of view. Science can't possibly capture the aesthetic and spiritual qualities of our world. Once these qualities become intellectualized, and given equations to represent their activity, they lose their essence. These aspects can never be explained; they can only be appreciated. Once you have explained the sunrise you've lost the sunrise. And once you have lost the sunrise you have lost God.

Appreciating the mysterious quality of the universe is the first of Heschel's ways to attain faith. The second is by sensing God through Torah. The revolutionary concepts alluded to by the Torah attest to its Divine origin. The Torah states, "In the beginning God created the heavens and the earth," and with that one dramatic proclamation altered the way man perceived the universe.

Jonathan Sacks explains that before Judaism, nature was viewed as innately inexplicable. Unable to account for natural disturbances like droughts or floods, the ancients attributed them to the blind rivalries of the gods who were integral parts of nature. The account of the creation of the world at the beginning of Genesis was a radical departure from this perspective. The Book of Genesis spoke of an infinitely powerful and wise force outside of nature that created our world. This completely new concept implies *a logical, comprehensible order to the universe.* Things no longer needed to be attributed the unfathomable whims of the gods. This allowed mankind to begin to explore nature and to shed rational light on its complexities: it was, ironically, the birth of science (*Radical Then, Radical Now*).

The Torah also altered the way mankind perceived itself. The claim at the beginning of Genesis that all men are created in the image of God has repercussions that are still being explored today. The notion that each person is an individual allows for the principles of the sanctity of human life, human rights, justice, and the concept of a free society. We need to look no further than the Declaration of Independence for a clear and concise statement of this concept:

> "We hold these truths to be self-evident, that all men are created equal, that they are endowed by their creator with certain unalienable rights, that among these are Life, Liberty and the Pursuit of happiness."

What few people appreciate is that when these ideas were first put forth by the Torah they were revolutionary. In ancient times, the kings were deemed gods and people were there to serve them. The elite classes maintained rights, not the general masses. There was a hierarchy of importance that was believed to be the natural order of things.

Stories in ancient times revolved around the hero – the godlike warrior, the king, the general. The Torah was the first book to discuss the family relationships and everyday struggles of ordinary people. The Torah was the first book to challenge the accepted ancient belief that people are inherently unequal, by emphasizing the importance of every human being (*Radical Then, Radical Now*).

The history writer Paul Johnson emphasizes this point in the epilogue of his book *History of the Jews*. He writes,

> One way of summing up 4,000 years of Jewish history is to ask ourselves what would have happened to the human race if . . . no specific Jewish people had come into being. . . . All the great conceptual discoveries of the intellect seem obvious and inescapable once they have been revealed, but it requires a special genius to formulate them for the first time. The Jews had this gift. To them we owe the idea of equality before the law, both Divine and human; of the sanctity of life and the dignity of the human person; of the individual conscience and so of personal redemption; of the collective conscience and so of social responsibility; of peace as an abstract ideal and love as the foundation of justice, and many other items which constitute the basic moral furniture of the human mind.

But it isn't only the uniquely powerful ideas embedded in the Torah that attest to its Divine character, it is also its history. The Jewish nation has miraculously survived two thousand years of inquisitions, pogroms, and a Holocaust, with no land, no common language, and no common culture. The same can be said of the Torah. The Torah has endured two thousand years of religious debates, book burnings, and exiles. And not only has it endured, it has given religion to more than half of the world, as well as having introduced the concepts of monotheism, human dignity, and equal justice into the global lexicon. No other book in human history can claim anything remotely similar. In the words of the French Emperor Napoleon Bonaparte: "The Bible is no mere book, but a Living Creature, with a power that conquers all that oppose it."

It often takes an outsider to show someone his own worth, particularly for self-deprecating Jews. But as Johnson, Napoleon and countless of others have observed, the history of the Jewish nation and the Torah defies logic to the extent that non-Jews just sit back and wonder. It isn't just the revolutionary ideas that the Torah has introduced into the world (albeit that would be enough), it's the very existence of the Torah and its unsurpassed influence on mankind that points to God.

Heschel's final method of sensing God is seeing Him in deeds. While Christianity is satisfied with its articles of faith, Judaism is centered around commandments: to act or to refrain from certain acts. Commandments serve to concretize faith, but they can also serve as a path to faith. How? According to Heschel, deeds in Judaism are metaphysical insights converted into an action. "By enacting the holy on the stage of concrete living, we perceive . . . the presence of the Divine. What cannot be grasped in reflection, we comprehend in deeds."

For Heschel, the commandments are Divine ideas made tangible. We can ascribe rationales for the laws, but they cannot come close to the depth of their true meaning. Acting out these laws brings us to an awareness of God.

Rabbi Soloveitchik illustrates this idea magnificently in his essay, "Majesty and Humility." Rabbi Soloveitchik explains that there is dichotomy within man. He is, on the one hand, majestic. His intellectual curiosity knows no bounds. He strives to gain knowledge of the vast cosmos. The deeper the mystery, the more motivated he is to solve it. He seeks God in galaxies billions of light years away. Man usually adopts this attitude in times of success.

But there is another aspect to man – humility. In times of sorrow, this is the dominant characteristic. Man becomes origin-oriented. He longs for home and seeks God in the tiny crevices of his physical space instead of the vast cosmos. He finds God in the "single spot of darkness which surrounds suffering man, from within black despair itself."

The Halacha (Jewish law) utilizes these attitudes to help shape man. Man cannot always be the victor. There are times when he must concede defeat. According to Rabbi Soloveitchik, this is a particular problem for modern man. Heschel, as well, pointed to it as one reason that modern man fails to see God: The inability to accept our limitations is ultimately detrimental to our souls.

The Halacha demands of man to retreat from one of his most treasured things: from his intellectual prowess. Halacha demands that man perform acts that he can't find reasons for – *Hukkim*. Halacha requires that man not mix meat and dairy, or wool and linen. Halacha tells man to separate from his wife when she is menstruating. The Halacha is full of rules that require man to suspend his intellectual inquisitiveness, and to admit defeat, so that he might become the type of person who can. These Halachot are the embodiment of this principle, and by performing them one becomes the type of person who can recognize God and live a life of holiness.

Faith is indeed elusive, but humanity has the means to acquire it. Experiencing the world instead of trying to explain it or utilize it for one's own purposes, learning about Torah values that have enlightened civilization for two thousand years, and performing the acts that are concretized conceptions of God's mind, are three ways to ever so softly graze the fingertips of God.

CHAPTER TWENTY-THREE

The Secret of Self Creation

FAITH CAN BE a powerful force. When it is used to advance personal gain, it has proven to be destructive and even deadly. But when it is used to advance the personal character of the individual, it signifies nothing less than the power of creation itself.

The ability to (re)create oneself is one of the most powerful abilities given to man. It allows him to become a partner with the Creator himself. According to Rabbi Soloveitchik, the ability to recreate oneself is one of the fundamental principles of Judaism.

A person's ability to decide her own fate has been debated since the origins of philosophy. Determinists, like Spinoza (as well as Einstein) claim that everything is pre-determined by nature ahead of time. Free Will is simply a construct of the human mind to compensate for the fact that we cannot predict the future. Some scientists have argued that man is simply the sum total of his heredity and pre-dispositions. His actions are the result of his pre-determined temperament. He doesn't define himself; he is born pre-defined, with the future already, to a large extent, in the past.

Many scientists adopt a more moderate view. Research has shown that man's genetic code alone can not accurately predict his actions or temperament. It is rather a combination of genes and experiences that mold man into who he turns out to be.

Judaism's definition of the concept of repentance redefines the notion of time, genetics, and causality, and goes one step further to give man complete Freedom of Will. As Rabbi Soloveitchik explains in *Halakhic Man*, the typical perception of time as linear doesn't apply to Judaism. The concept of linear time dictates a past, a present, and a future with one-dimensional causation; the past can dictate the future, but the future can't effect the past. There is essentially nothing we can do about our past experiences. They are there simply to define us. Essentially, man becomes a victim of his past.

But the Jewish notion of repentance rectifies this situation. It allows man to completely overcome his past, in effect changing it, completely re-creating himself in the process.

In Judaism, a person's past sins can be altered by his present good deeds. Sins can not only be overcome, but even used to catapult oneself to greater heights. Past sins can be retroactively transformed to present good deeds, and future great ones, if they are used as opportunities to learn and grow as a human being. With this ability to change one's past experiences into tools of development, human beings are empowered to completely alter themselves. Genes don't define us. Our experiences can't even completely define us. We define ourselves. This is Judaism's secret: self creation.

The biblical narrative has God putting man and woman on this earth and commanding them not only to procreate, but, according to Traditional Jewish commentaries, to re-create themselves.

And this gift doesn't just work with repentance. Once man has been given the opportunity to re-create himself, it opens the door for other experiences to alter him. Heart surgery, family tragedies, or even the birth of a child, are all life experiences that man can use to propel himself to new heights.

I remember the moment of the birth of my first son. The tension in the room was palpable. "Push!" I heard as I squeezed my eyes shut and tried to block out the pain and the incessant bleeps from the monitor. "The baby's oxygen level is dangerously low," I heard the nurse explain to my husband, as she pushed me over to my left side after I had pushed. Please be okay, I found myself pleading to my unborn child. I felt like I was in a compression chamber. My brain was pounding so hard in my head, I could barely hear the tens of medical personnel surrounding my bed. And then with one final push – all was silent. It was like a bubble floating across the room; it was a fragile fleeting moment of magic – the moment a new life enters this world, and then POP! The spell was broken.

The pediatricians grabbed the baby and started to suction his lungs. I was relieved and elated, yet concerned and impatient all at once. I looked over to the small bed where my tiny new son lay, barely visible through the screen of hovering doctors and nurses. I wanted to scream, "Leave him alone!"

"When will they let him breathe?" I heard myself asking the obstetrician who was busily taking care of me, hardly noticing what was going on in the next bed. She looked over at them, but before she could speak, a loud cry pierced through the air – finally! mercifully! – trumpeting my son's safe arrival into the world. They congratulated me, wiped him off, and gave him a clean bill of health. The next thing I knew I was holding a soft, warm package wrapped in a cotton white blanket in my bended arm.

I was enveloped by an overwhelming feeling of peace as I examined his precious features. I ran my fingers over his translucent eyebrows – they were barely there at all! I tried to make eye contact with his silver-blue eyes, but my own eyes melted at the sight of them. I felt the soft bump of his tiny nose and the ever-so-slight curve of his mouth, and I took the deepest sigh I had ever taken. I hadn't even noticed the doctors making their abrupt departures and the nurses smiling at my husband while they tiptoed out of the room. I hardly even noticed my husband, who must have been in his own private world of bliss.

I hugged my new son gently and wondered for the hundredth time what kind of mother I'd be. There were so many different kinds of mothers. There were strict ones, soft-hearted ones, neurotic ones (I knew I'd be that sort!), and laid-back ones. There were mothers whose whole lives revolved around their children – happily, and then there were mothers who made it a point not to let that happen. There was no motherhood manual. I briefly wondered what my mother had been like before she gave birth to my oldest brother. Was she always the same selfless, loving woman? Probably not, I decided, as I looked over to the tiny bundle that lay in the crook of my arm. *From now on, it's you and me, kid*, I found myself thinking. I was unaware of the degree of truth of this statement.

I was no longer an "I. " I had become, then and forever, a "We." I took another deep sigh and closed my exhausted eyes without letting go – the steadiness in my arm and the closed position of my eyes had become automatically disassociated, a mechanism familiar to many a new mother. Unbeknownst to me at the time, two people were created that afternoon – my precious son, now drifting into a peaceful slumber, and the grateful, exhausted mother, ready to jump at the slightest stir.

I was permanently changed that day in Columbia Presbyterian Hospital. But there was this: *Who I became was determined by me. I* ultimately decided what kind of mother I was becoming. God gave me the experience and told me to make something out of it. He told me to create myself in an image of my choice. A scientist might have said that I was destined to become my own mother. I had her genes. I watched her mother me. I inherited her sense of humor, her intelligence, and her (unhealthy) need for cleanliness. Science could only account for the things I did just like my mother. But it couldn't account for the decisions I'd make that she didn't. It couldn't account for my individuality. Only something in my own spirit would give me the power to be me, and mother that way. Only my own faith in my own path would provide me with the ability to completely re-create myself as I sought to parent this new child. And only *his* individuality would allow him to both obey and defy me over the years, the latter at an intensity that would sometimes make me forget the warm fuzziness of the day that sweet package arrived. Science can't account for that degree of Free Will; God gave it to me as a gift.

By the Light of the Moon

"Mommy, what's this?" I heard my three-year-old son ask me, as we sat together reading *Clifford the Big Red Dog* on the living room rug. I looked over at him to see what he was pointing to. He was looking at his leg.

"That's a scab."

"Oh." Then a small pause before, "What's a scab?"

"Well, Honey, you must have had a boo-boo on your leg, and now it's getting better. In order for your body to fix itself it makes scabs." I silently congratulated myself on that answer. Dr. Spock would be proud, I thought.

He started to pick it off.

"Don't take it off, sweetie, that's your body's way of healing itself. If you pick it off, it'll just grow back," I explained.

"Oh . . . Mommy, you have a boo-boo too."

I looked over at him for a minute, and noticed that he was pointing at my leg. It was the leg that was covered with the skin graft.

"Is your body going to make a scab, Mommy?" He asked.

"No, Honey, Mommy's body won't be making a scab to fix this boo-boo," I answered.

"Aren't you going to get better?" My son wanted to know.

I didn't know what to say.

For a moment, I looked at the graft. I had become so accustomed to it over the years that sometimes I forgot it was there. But I wanted to try to see what he saw. It was bigger than most grafts. It was, in fact, four grafts that covered my knee and about two inches above it. Because there was no layer of fat to pull the skin off the bone, the skin clung to my knee, making it possible to see the protruding boney parts beneath it. It reminded me of the brown gloves my mother used to wear. They hugged her skin so tightly that I could clearly see the bumps of her knuckles through the soft leather. The color of the graft wasn't contiguous. It was a mixture between the red shades of raw injured skin, and the peachy brown shades of skin that want to be skin color, but don't quite make it. It didn't feel like normal skin either. Some sections were smooth and bumpy – like the skin of a viper. Other sections were prickly and scratchy – like the back of a rough-skinned lizard. There was even a section that never really "took" properly which had circular indentations in it: the branding of the fateful taxi that hit me on that rainy spring day. The crazy thing is, I CAN fix it, I thought. But I don't want to.

When I was first told about the ability to remove the skin graft, I turned it down, because I was not interested in another hospital procedure. I had just come out of the hospital a few weeks prior, and the scents of alcohol and IV drips were still in my nose. I had no interest in partaking of them again. So I went home with my good-enough graft, and learned how to adjust. Perhaps I did too good a job, because it really didn't bother me anymore. Sometimes, late at night, when exhaustion had just begun to take hold of me, so that I was not yet tired enough to fall asleep, but was completely and totally relaxed, I would look at my knee. It was at these moments that I came to see the graft by a new light – by the light of the moon as opposed to the light of the sun.

I liked the way the scar that snaked its way above the graft was silvery white, like the color of my grandmother's pearl necklace. And I liked the way the upper portion of the graft was soft and mushy. It reminded me of the bottom of a baby's foot, with its texture and combination of pinks, peaches, and subtle shades of white. I liked the feel of the tiny bumps created by the braiding of the fine layers of skin that make up the graft. The bumps formed a pattern across my leg, similar to one you might find on your cheek after you've fallen asleep for a few hours on a knitted afghan. I liked how the various shades of pink, red, peach, and white were dispersed softly throughout the graft. No one color dominated. They were all mixed together to form a brand new hue that didn't yet exist in a color catalogue. But mostly, I liked the fact that the graft reminded me of my faith in God with all its complexities.

♦   ♦   ♦

Job sighed as he turned back toward his tent. He would later become a man with a mission. He would pray for his friends, create a new family, and move on with his life. He would never forget what he lost, though. Late at night when the moon created pale shadows with the trees, he'd think about his lost children. He'd remember the way they joked with each other, and the way they tried to get out of their chores. He'd remember the meeting he had with God and the answers he did and did not receive. He'd remember the hard-earned lessons of faith.

Elihu took a long, deep breath as he put away his writing materials. His *Book of Job* was complete. He sat and stared for a while at the pages in front of him. Writing it had brought back agonizing memories. He was a little surprised by how exhausted he felt after reliving the events of the destruction of the Temple in Jerusalem. And then there were those rare moments of emotional clarity when he could admit that it wasn't just the Temple he was thinking about, it was his lost family . . .

As he slowly rose from his writing table, he briefly wondered if readers would surmise the truth about the *Book of Job*. He wondered if people would suspect that its self-assured author was also its tormented main character.

ABOUT THE AUTHOR

CHERYL BERMAN is a teacher and writer with the unique ability to communicate complex dilemmas of faith in relevant and pragmatic terms. After earning her Masters Degree in Medieval Jewish Philosophy from Bernard Revel Graduate School, Berman went on to teach Jewish Philosophy in various institutions of learning in New York and Israel. She now writes and teaches Jewish Philosophy in Israel, where she lives with her family. Visit her website at www.Reasonable-Doubts.com, where you can read more of her work and join the community discussions of this book.